WASHINGTON ART

*A Guide to Galleries,
Art Consultants, and Museums*

WASHINGTON ART

*A Guide to Galleries,
Art Consultants, and Museums*

by

Lorraine Arden   *Carolyn Blakeslee*   *Drew Steis*

*published by
Art Calendar
Great Falls, Virginia*

Dedicated to Washington artists, all of whom are talented and unique, without whom there would be no D.C. art to speak of; the dealers, all of whom are art historians and characters of the best kind, without whom there would be no easy way to find art; the critics, without whom there would be lesser standards; and the collectors, without whom there would be no market. Thanks to all of you for helping us prepare this book.

Copyright © 1988 by *Art Calendar*.

All Rights Reserved.

No part of this publication may be reproduced, stored in a retrieval or information system, or transmitted, in any form or by any means, electronic, mechanical, photocopied, recorded, or otherwise, without the prior written permission of the publisher.

All information contained in *Washington Art* was current and correct at the time of publication. However, the nature of guidebooks and directories is that information gradually becomes out of date. Please send comments, changes, additions, and deletions to the publisher, as new editions may be published every several years.

Published by
Art Calendar
Post Office Box 1040
Great Falls, VA 22066

ISBN 0-945388-00-4

Printed in the United States of America.

Cover Illustration: *Crossing Paths*, 1987, by J. Seward Johnson, Jr. Cast bronze with color patinas, lifesize. Sculpture Placement, page 169.

Cover Design by Beverly Schroeder, Schroeder Graphics, Great Falls, Virginia.

CONTENTS

FOREWORD 6

INTRODUCTION

For the Collector 7
   Collecting in Washington
   Art of Historic and Ethnic Interest
   Contemporary Artists
   For the Beginning Collector: About Prints
   Summary

*For the Artist Seeking Gallery Representation
for the First Time* 9
   Before You Approach a Gallery
   Your Portfolio
   Business Arrangements
   Summary

GALLERIES—CONTEMPORARY ART 11

   Commercial: Primarily Contemporary Art 12
   Cooperative: Contemporary Art 73
   Commercial: Functional Art 86
   Commercial: Multiples and More 93

**GALLERIES—ART OF HISTORIC
AND/OR ETHNIC SIGNIFICANCE** 100

   Commercial: Historical Art 101
   Commercial: Art of Other Cultures, All Time Periods 112

MUSEUMS 117

OTHER SPACES EXHIBITING ART 143

   Art Centers 144
   College and University Art Galleries 153
   Alternative Spaces 155

ART CONSULTANTS 159

INDEX 171

FOREWORD

Combine the elements of thousands of talented local artists; an abundance of substantive, thoughtful, sound criticism; dealers who have or can acquire any kind of fine art by any artist; dealers continually reviewing new work; active and interested collectors; and some of the most renowned and best attended museums in the world. The result is Washington, a major art center.

During the last 10 years the art scene in Washington has changed dramatically. New galleries and museums have opened. Many established galleries have moved, expanded, or changed their focus and/or the artists they represent. The increasing trend toward corporate collecting and public art has also revitalized the market.

Amid this whirlwind of activity, where do you find what you want? How does a collector find a gallery that suits his or her personality and needs? How and where does an artist find gallery representation?

This book was written with two goals in mind:

• To provide a comprehensive overview of the art scene in the Washington area, thereby creating a useful directory and guide book for collectors, artists, dealers, and visitors. Although many excellent publications offer monthly listings of current shows, there is not room in them to tell what the galleries stand for, and what kind of work they generally handle. People are too busy to visit the hundreds of art sources in Washington just to find out what kind of art each dealer offers. This book gives you that information.

• To clarify for artists which of the galleries are open to reviewing new work, what their interests are, and how to submit a portfolio for review. For years, artists have been in the dark about how to approach galleries. These pages will clarify procedures, protocol, and the facts of dealing with the dealers.

In early 1987 we sent a detailed questionnaire to every gallery listed in this book. We asked some tough questions, and the completed questionnaires were a good start. Then, if we had not visited the gallery before, we dropped in on every gallery profiled here to see for ourselves, to ensure that the book would be as comprehensive and accurate as possible. Sometimes several follow-up telephone calls were necessary as well.

Each gallery was categorized according to its main focus. However, because most galleries are unique spaces which offer a variety of work, there is of necessity some overlap. A few of the categorizations were difficult choices.

We hope this book gives you the information necessary to find a gallery or cluster of galleries showing work which suits you. Your comments are welcome.

Lorraine Arden   Carolyn Blakeslee   Drew Steis

INTRODUCTION

FOR THE COLLECTOR

Collecting in Washington

When you buy from a gallery that supports contemporary Washington artists, you are helping Washington to develop its own distinctive art. The more distinguished regional art is, and the more popular it is, the more attention it earns, and the more valuable it becomes. When you buy from a Washington gallery that supports contemporary artists from other areas, you contribute to the area becoming all the more attractive. More artists from other areas send their work here, and the best art rises to the top. When you patronize a gallery dealing in art of other periods and cultures, you still distinguish Washington art, because it enriches the art world to have this variety available.

You, the collector, are a vital part of the Washington art scene.

Washington offers an ample supply of accomplished dealers with curatorial skills. Are you looking for an Old Master or an O'Keeffe or a Rosenquist? Someone in Washington either has it already or is equipped to acquire if for you. Would you prefer the thrill of "discovering" an emerging artist and contributing to his/her career? Especially promising young artists appear on the Washington scene regularly.

You are "an important collector." The Washington art dealers and consultants may be willing to go the extra mile while the dealers in New York and other art centers may consider your business to be routine. Art dealers are happy to work with you and your budget; most dealers are very open and friendly when sincere interest is shown in their artists. It is in their interests too that their artists become all the more established, and many of them consider it an honor to educate people. Many dealers are willing to work out payment plans, lease/purchase arrangements, even the "live with it for a week" option. Most of them are sympathetic to the fears people have when they buy art, but a good dealer will work with you to find a piece which will make you wonder how you ever could have doubted.

Acquisitions aside, some of the area's dealers are highly skilled, experienced appraisers and are happy to advise or assist clients wishing to sell certain artworks.

Art of Historic and Ethnic Interest

As you might expect in a city of history, politics, and important museums, a wide variety of historical art is available. This is a city of diplomats and world travelers. Many galleries have opened which specialize in the art of other cultures—African, Asian, Greek, Polish, Hispanic, even Eskimo. Also, in a city where news happens every minute and is photographed, there are several galleries specializing in or heavily emphasizing contemporary photography. Political cartoons are available as well.

Museums here offer an abundance of services. Some of the finest exhibits in the world are installed in Washington art institutions. But sometimes of more immediate relevance, the collector's most valuable resources—curators and conservators—are open to being of assistance. Restorers and appraisers can be recommended, and assistance in authentication is often extended.

Contemporary Artists

Washington boasts more than its share of major artists. Works by Sam Gilliam, Willem de Looper, the late Gene Davis, the late Leon Berkowitz, and other Washington Color School figures, are readily available. Rockne Krebs, a sculptor working with lasers, enjoys a national reputation. William Willis, William Christenberry, and several other nationally known southern artists are living and working in D.C. Kenneth Marlow, Joseph Sheppard, and Will Wilson—three of the best artists working in traditional realism today—live within a half-hour of the city. In a recent nationwide competition sponsored by *American Artist*, over a tenth of the artists selected were in the D.C. area—New Yorkers were actually less prevalent.

Over 10,000 artists live here. Many create art on a part-time basis and consider themselves to be "emerging," which means that you may be able to acquire a quality contemporary piece at a relatively low price.

Art centers and alternative spaces—that is, galleries often organized by artists as alternatives to commercial galleries—generally feature changing group and solo shows. These spaces often show work which is provocative or controversial.

For the Beginning Collector: About Prints

Artists often put in hundreds of hours on a piece; "relatively low price" or "bargain" may seem high-priced to some people, but it could mean minimum wage or less for the artist.

If one-of-a-kind art is beyond your budget, you might wish to consider multiples, from original prints to posters. "Original print" means a limited edition print which has been hand-pulled, signed, and numbered by the artist. "Hand-pulled" means the artist, or a master printer, actually produced the print him/herself, as opposed to an automated photo-offset process utilizing color separations of a photograph of an original artwork. The color plates in this book, while they are a form of large-edition multiple, were produced using the latter process. "Limited edition" means that only a few—say, 125—pieces like the one you are considering buying exist. The number written by hand on the edge of the print image tells you what the edition number was. For example, 13/125 means you have the 13th print pulled from an edition of 125. Posters and photo-offset prints, on the other hand, exist in theoretically unlimited number and are therefore less expensive but perhaps less valuable. Photo-offset prints including posters are recognizable under fine scrutiny; if squinted at for a few seconds, tiny dots of pure color will become discernible.

Summary: The General Scene

Good criticism keeps the art world on its toes. Regionally and nationally respected art writers actively produce written opinion in Washington. Major art publications, some distributed nationally, have established editorial offices in Washington. *New Art Examiner* is a national magazine which was founded to critically analyze new artists, movements, even art publications. *Washington Review, Museum & Arts Washington,* and the *Washington Post* and *Washington Times* publish reviews by major art critics. *ARTnews* and *Art in America* list Washington editors on their mastheads. Also based in the area, *Art Calendar*—this book's publisher—produces a monthly newsletter listing upcoming local, national, and international professional opportunities for visual artists.

Whatever your choice of medium or subject matter, whatever your budget, the art you seek is available in Washington. The research you do will be fun and informative, and you will be sure to find people with whom you enjoy working and even socializing.

FOR THE ARTIST
SEEKING GALLERY REPRESENTATION
FOR THE FIRST TIME

Before You Approach a Gallery

This book tells you what kind of work the local galleries are handling, whether they are interested in representing any additional artists, and if so how an artist may submit work. But you must be prepared.

The foundation of being a successful artist is respecting your own work. When you are producing consistent work which you really like, in a direction you are excited about, then you are ready to share it with the public.

Art dealers are people too; they like it when an applicant artist is genuinely interested in showing at that particular gallery—when an artist comes in with some knowledge about their philosophies and show approaches—as opposed to just getting a gallery, any gallery. Attending shows regularly will bring many benefits: the local art scene will become your own knowledge and not just hearsay. You will see for yourself the quality of work represented, the extent of the galleries' advertising, and the sort of press coverage they generate. You will meet important people.

Build a list of galleries with which you are interested in exhibiting. You might put these galleries on your personal mailing list and send them invitations to any shows in which you are participating. Add collectors, curators, and critics to your list too; these people will become familiar with your name. Add other artists you respect to your list as you meet them—you never know when a referral might result.

While you do your research, prepare your slides and portfolio.

Your Portfolio

Make sure your slides are truly representative of your work. The color saturation should be perfect, slide images should be squarely composed with no interfering background, and the slide labels and accompanying slide identification sheet should be neatly typed. A professional slide photographer will be able to assist you.

Treat yourself to a neatly prepared portfolio book. Since the dealer is him/herself a professional salesperson, it is your work, not a sales pitch, which counts; presenting your work clearly and neatly will help you. A good portfolio book includes a current resumé, a brief artist's statement, press materials—even ads—photographs of some of your artworks, and slides.

If you are calling the gallery for an appointment to show your portfolio, offer to bring a couple of original pieces if they are portable enough. If you are sending them slides and a resumé, always enclose a self-addressed stamped envelope (SASE). These considerations are appreciated. SASE's also ensure that you will get your slides back.

It is possible that you will be turned down once, twice, or several times before you contract with a gallery. Although it could be painful, *do not give up;* if your work is solid and presented well there is a dealer for you. Most dealers are always looking for new work even though they are often booked up to two years in advance.

Business Arrangements

Our questions to the galleries about their business arrangements elicited fairly uniform responses, so we are covering those matters here generally, rather than dealing with each individual gallery's policies. What follows are some usual policies. Terms vary, of course, from gallery to gallery.

Most gallery directors prefer a written agreement between the gallery and the artist. Specific policies should be addressed at contract time. Many of the galleries openly said that their agreements and terms vary from artist to artist—for example, sometimes exclusive area representation is arranged, other times it is not a requirement. When asked whether an artist owes the gallery a commission from work sold from the artist's studio, many gallery directors answered, "It depends."

The main thing to remember here is that no professional art dealers we know of are out to deliberately take advantage of their artists and clients. Granted, they all intend to make money; but if they acquire a reputation of not paying artists in a timely manner or not at all, or of dealing with clients unfairly or dishonestly, they hopefully will not be in business for long. If you trust your instincts and take care of contractual arrangements in an objective and up-front way, your association with your dealer will be happy, hopefully long, and mutually productive.

Commissions run about 50%, give or take. The cost of mounting an exhibition really is very high. Starting with rent, staff salary, spackling and painting after each show, and moving on through printed matter, advertising and promotion, and receptions, the gallery business is not for the faint-hearted. Overhead can run thousands of dollars per show. Sometimes when discounts are agreed upon the discount comes out of the commission, sometimes not. Make sure terms are understood. If they are not mutually agreeable and clear, no one will be happy.

Directors will help you with pricing; they know what the market will bear.

Work is almost always insured while at the gallery.

Usually the artist is responsible for some or all of the framing, and for transporting the work to and from the gallery. The gallery almost always foots the bill for a fairly nice opening reception for your show.

Although galleries send out news releases announcing shows, it behooves the artist to send out releases too. The old saw, "The squeaky wheel gets the oil," can apply. Make sure critics also receive an invitation to your show opening.

Most Washington galleries list in *galleries* magazine, the monthly publication giving current show information, as well as other magazines and newspapers. But display ads including a black-and-white photograph start at just $40. Even color ads are not out of reach. However, lead time is one to four months before publication. Usually the gallery is willing to pay for some advertising within reason, sometimes they ask to share the costs. Make sure the ad image and copy is mutually agreeable.

Usually the gallery will pay for the printing of several hundred show announcement/invitations. The gallery pays for postage to their mailing list, and the artist is responsible for postage to his/her list. Sometimes a catalog can assist in the selling of your work, but fancy catalogs are not usually produced for a first show.

Summary: The Long Run

Ideally the relationship between artist and dealer will develop and grow. As together you establish the saleability and reputation of your work, the gallery will gradually bear more costs. Gallery staff will prove themselves to you as they make sales and pay you promptly. You will prove yourself to them at the same time. Do not call every day to see if anything has sold; you may be interrupting a sale.

A good art dealer is concerned about short-run sales, yet will be interested in representing you for many years. S/he may help you obtain placement in galleries in other cities, in museum collections, and in corporate and private collections. You are in a business partnership together; s/he is not your boss, nor is s/he your employee. But one cannot exist without the other. Respect your relationship with your dealer and your buyers, and love the contribution to the arts which only you can make.

GALLERIES SHOWING PRIMARILY CONTEMPORARY ART

Commercial/Contemporary
Cooperative/Contemporary
Commercial/Functional
Commercial/Multiples and More

Contemporary

Simplicity, 1986,
by Javier Cabada.
Acrylic on canvas, 7'x5 1/2'.
Aaron Gallery.

AARON GALLERY

1717 Connecticut Avenue, N.W.
Washington, DC 20009
(202)234-3311
Tuesday-Saturday 10-6,
Sunday 2-6

Owner: Annette K. Aaron
Director: Consuelo C. Aaron
Price Range: $500-15,000
Cash, check, payment plan
Established 1970

Aaron, originally established here in 1970, re-opened in Washington in 1986 after a stint in SoHo.

Aaron Gallery handles contemporary paintings and sculpture by American artists, emerging as well as established professionals. The large Dupont Circle space is capable of housing up to two solo shows as well as a group show at the same time. Aaron's capability extends into the arena of large-scale pieces, too; paintings and tapestries are available, as well as steel installations for interiors or out-of-doors.

MEDIA: Paintings, drawings, sculpture, original prints, collage.

STYLES: Generally abstract, including expressionist, abstract-expressionist, lyrical expressionist, and conceptual.

ARTISTS REGULARLY SHOWN: Artist list includes: James Havens (stainless steel sculpture), Hy Suchman (steel sculpture), Michael Kligerman (bronzes), Javier Cabada (paintings), Shirley Smith, Charles Schucker.

SELECTION OF NEW ARTISTS: Artists may send slides with a resumé and recommendations, or phone for an appointment. New artists are selected based on originality, consistency, and professionalism. Shows are scheduled up to a year in advance.

A SALON

Please refer to the next chapter, Cooperative Galleries.

DAVID ADAMSON GALLERY

406 7th Street, N.W.
Washington, DC 20004
(202)628-0257
Tuesday-Saturday 10-5
Member Washington Art Dealers Association
and Printmakers Council, London

Owner: David Adamson
Director: Laurie Hughs
Cash, check
Established 1982

In the 406 Building, David Adamson Gallery is on the third floor next to the McIntosh/Drysdale Gallery. Ambience is friendly—even if they are installing a show, their door is open—and staff is willing to explain.

A master printmaker, British-born and -educated David Adamson is a practicing professional artist himself. He has expanded his printmaking skills into the field of computer-assisted images, generally manifesting in their final form as large-scale paintings which are often portraits.

Adamson shows a wide range of work by painters and printmakers. Both an artist and a dealer, he wishes to be sensitive to the issues which both people may have in working with each other. He and Laurie Hughs express the hope that they "create and develop a greater understanding and respect among the artist, dealer, and the collecting public."

MEDIA: Paintings, works on paper, original prints, sculpture.

STYLES: Realist work with a twist—figurative to photorealist to pop.

ARTISTS REGULARLY SHOWN: 15-20 artists are shown in a given year, including: William Newman (Remember the nude Sara murals inside construction sites? Newman's relatively small-scale work can be found here); Kevin MacDonald (hauntingly personless land- and urbanscapes); Catherine Satterlee (large, loosely-painted canvases of place settings). Work by many other artists is available as well.

SELECTION OF NEW ARTISTS: Artists may send a letter with resumé and slides; new artists are chosen with regard to originality and content, proficiency of technique, and consistency. Shows are scheduled four months to a year or more in advance.

ADDISON/RIPLEY GALLERY

9 Hillyer Court, N.W.
Washington, DC 20008
(202)328-2332
Tuesday-Saturday 11-5
Member Washington Art Dealers Association,
  Dupont Circle Fine Art Galleries

Owner/Directors: Christopher Addison
and Sylvia Ripley
Price Range: $250-25,000
Cash, check, payment plan
Established 1981

The Addison/Ripley Gallery is difficult to find but worth the effort. The gallery is in a spacious carriage house, in a courtyard in the middle of a triangular block bounded by 21st Street, R Street, and Florida Avenue. The Cosmos Club is somewhere in there too.

A husband and wife team, Christopher Addison and Sylvia Ripley were trained as conservators; each has a degree in studio art. They like to show both emerging and well-known artists. Some of the shows Addison/Ripley sponsors embrace unusual or traditionally ignored media, such as "The Quiltmaker as Artist: Nine Artists from New York." The artwork here is always well-crafted and striking.

Part of the upstairs is occupied by the Foundry Gallery, an artists' cooperative.

MEDIA: Paintings, drawings, sculpture, photography, original prints, collage, installations.

STYLES: Representational; impressionist; abstract including expressionist, abstract-expressionist, minimalist, experimental, Washington Color School, conceptual. Commissions can be arranged.

ARTISTS REGULARLY SHOWN: Rebecca Cross, Michael Smallwood, Dickson Carroll, William Noland (bronze, polychromed wood, steel abstract sculpture), Edith Kuhnle, Jonathan Shahn, Mel Watkin (large-scale surrealist drawings, dream themes).

SELECTION OF NEW ARTISTS: Artists may send slides with a resumé; new artists are chosen based on originality, consistency, and technique. Shows are scheduled a year or two in advance. The gallery sponsors new talent shows.

Paestum (Poseidon), 1986, by David Lowe. Charcoal and conté on paper, 78"x98". AFR Fine Art.

AFR FINE ART

2030 R Street, N.W.
Washington, DC 20009
(202)265-6191
Tuesday-Saturday 11-5:30

Owner/Director: Andrea Ruggieri
Price Range: $500-10,000
Cash, check, payment plan
Established 1986

Located on the R Street gallery corridor, AFR Fine Art's entrance is below street level. A small two-room gallery, this well-lit English basement space is nonetheless cleanly designed, with an interior architecture which makes it seem bigger. A charming cupola with natural light serves as one of the exhibit areas in the front gallery.

This gallery shows a variety of contemporary artwork of consistently high quality by artists known and emerging. Works on paper may be seen in a show with paintings and sculpture, yet they work together. The next show could present large-scale, loosely-drawn charcoal drawings of classical architecture. Yet all the different approaches to work handled at AFR reflect Andrea Ruggieri's commitment to "showing artwork that is intellectually and emotionally challenging."

MEDIA: Sculpture, paintings, works on paper, original prints.

STYLES: Representational, abstract, abstract expressionist, minimalist, spiritual. Commissions can be arranged.

ARTISTS REGULARLY SHOWN: Ruggieri brings in work from around the world, especially by artists from New York and the Washington area: works on paper by Susan Rothenberg, Jim Dine, Eric Fischl, and Robert Kushner; works on paper and paintings by David Lowe, Lucy Clark, Raymond Charneau, Sally Gilbert, and others.

SELECTION OF NEW ARTISTS: Artists are selected based on consistency, originality/content, and clarity of vision. Interested artists may send a letter with slides, a resumé, and recommendations. Open jury days are Thursday and Friday mornings. Shows are currently scheduled up to one year in advance.

Approach, Together, Meeting,
1987,
by Hans Versteeg.
Bronze and brass,
approx. 26" in height.
Alex Gallery.

ALEX GALLERY

2106 R Street, N.W.
Washington, DC 20008
(202) 667-2599
Tuesday-Saturday 11-5

Owner/Director: Victor Gaetan
Cash, check, payment plan
Established 1987

European born Victor Gaetan has an M.A. in international law, and a Ph.D. in French literature. Not surprisingly, his brand-new gallery has an international focus. Alex Gallery handles relatively freely executed work by contemporary American, Canadian, and European artists. Gaetan wishes to "encourage the exchange of ideas and styles in artistic creation." So far the work shown here has been strong, attractive, and reasonably priced.

In a townhouse on the R Street gallery corridor, the gallery has a beautiful sweeping interior. Hardwood floors, high ceilings, understated architectural detail, and rooms which feel very large make possible the exhibition of many kinds of art in many scales.

MEDIA: Paintings, sculpture, drawings.

STYLES: Representational, figurative, impressionist, abstract, expressionist, abstract-expressionist. Commissions can be arranged.

ARTISTS REGULARLY SHOWN: Martine Vaugel (currently director of sculpture, New York Academy of Art; erotic cast sculpture); Erik Slutsky (representational paintings with an expressionist edge); Catharina Biddle, Thomas O'Callaghan (Washington painters); Kari Walden (Finnish painter); Hans Veersteeg (Dutch sculptor); Andrea Bove (Swiss sculptor); Patrick Matheus (American sculptor).

SELECTION OF NEW ARTISTS: Artists interested in showing at Alex may send slides and a resumé, or phone for an appointment. Artists will be selected based on professionalism of presentation, originality, and consistency. New talent shows will be sponsored. Shows are scheduled six months or more in advance.

ALPHA GALLERY

176 Rollins Avenue
Rockville, MD 20852
(301)231-7388
Monday-Saturday 10-6

Owner/Directors: Barbara Loftin
and Eric Moe
Cash, check, MasterCard, Visa,
American Express, payment plan
Established 1985

    Alpha Gallery is a suburban storefront gallery and frame shop just off Rockville Pike.
    Alpha shows a wide variety of artwork by local artists. The gallery aspect of their business is informal—they change the work on exhibit when they feel like it—but the one-of-a-kind work is usually quality work worthy of attention.
    Besides custom framing, art consulting services are offered.
    MEDIA: Paintings, drawings, original prints, sculpture, signed offsets, photography, jewelry, ceramics, architectural.
    STYLES: Relatively conservative: representational, impressionist. Commissions can be arranged.
    ARTISTS REGULARLY SHOWN: Nancy Denison, Azoulay, Segoavia, Earl Biss, Embroli, Frank Howell, Martineau, Catherine O'Connor.
    SELECTION OF NEW ARTISTS: Artists are welcome to call for an appointment.

AMERICANA WEST GALLERY

1630 Connecticut Avenue, N.W.
Washington, DC 20009
(202)255-1630
Monday-Saturday 10-8,
    Sunday 12-5

Owner: Leslie Stone
Director: Lyn Hackworth
Cash, check, MasterCard, Visa,
American Express
Established 1986

    Americana West Gallery, in the space formerly occupied by Midtown Galleries, is one of the few galleries in the city which handles the work of native American and Western artists.
    No clichés here. Along with paintings and limited edition prints, traditional and authentic native American art is available, like Acoma pottery, as well as Zuni, Navaho, Hopi, Pueblo, and Chippewa work. Leslie Stone and Lyn Hackworth have managed to stay away from squash blossom necklaces and such.
    MEDIA: Traditional native American work, and western-influenced work, including paintings, drawings, ceramics, original prints, signed offsets, sculpture, jewelry.
    STYLES: Western themes in a diverse range of styles including traditional, impressionist, expressionist, and abstract; also traditional Native American styles.
    ARTISTS REGULARLY SHOWN: Alyce Frank (oil paintings), Jeffrey Zigulis (saggar fired pots), Presley and Bruce La Fountain (Utah alabaster sculpture), R. C. Gorman, Earl Biss, Amado Peña (lithographs), Wesley Anderegg (raku pottery), Ben Nighthorse Campbell (Congressman from Colorado who makes bracelets), Anthony Sanchez (silver pieces with inlaid semiprecious stones).
    SELECTION OF NEW ARTISTS: Artists working in the appropriate styles may send a letter with resumé and slides. New artists are chosen based on consistency, proficiency of technique, and saleability.

Pensée, 1986, by Gigi Guadagnucci. Carrara marble, $19^1/2$" in height. Andreas Galleries.

ANDREAS GALLERIES

2904 M Street, N.W.
Washington, DC 20007
(202)337-2000
Monday-Friday 9:30-6:30,
Saturday-Sunday 12-6

Owner: Ursula Andreas
Director: Laura Craig
Cash, check, MasterCard, Visa,
American Express, payment plan
Established 1983

"Tasteful" is the word that comes to mind when talking about Andreas Gallery. This well-appointed, subdued gallery is the setting where contemporary European and American work is on exhibit.

European-born Ursula Andreas and her staff also offer art consulting services. Additional work can be seen by appointment at two other locations.

MEDIA: Primarily paintings and sculpture; occasionally drawings, handmade paper, original prints.

STYLES: Representational; impressionist; abstract including expressionist, minimalist, abstract expressionist; surrealist. Commissions can be arranged.

ARTISTS REGULARLY SHOWN: Trevor Southey (humanistic paintings, sculpture, graphics), Primo Conti (Italian futurist), Salvatore Fimme, Lloyd Kelly (colorist; equestrian themes), Birgitta Ara (Scandinavian sculptor; bronze and marble works with romantic themes); Gigi Guadagnucci (Italian marble sculptor).

SELECTION OF NEW ARTISTS: Artists may send a letter with resumé, recommendations and slides. New artists are chosen based primarily on originality and proficiency of technique.

ANTON GALLERY

2108 R Street, N.W.
Washington, DC 20008
(202)328-0828
Tuesday-Saturday 12-5
and by appointment
Member Washington Art Dealers Association
and Dupont Circle Fine Art Galleries

Owner: Gail Enns
Director: John Gustave Figura
Cash, check, MasterCard, Visa, payment plan
Established 1981

Anton Gallery is a spacious, light-filled gallery consisting of several rooms on two levels of a townhouse near Dupont Circle.

Gail Enns likes showing art of a high quality while encouraging a progressive, risk-taking point of view. She views the gallery as a forum for the activity of the process of art. In fact, a practicing professional artist serves as her gallery director.

While generally exhibiting work of an expressionist bent, occasionally Anton sponsors an entirely different kind of show. For example, this gallery put on an exhibit of naive art when the Corcoran's folk/naive show was on view.

MEDIA: Paintings, sculpture, works on paper, original prints.

STYLES: New abstract and figurative work. Commissions can be arranged.

ARTISTS REGULARLY SHOWN: Tom Nakashima (prints, figurative paintings with social commentary, Japanese Byobu folding screens), John Figura (allegorical paintings), Al Carter (sometimes whimsical paintings and constructions), Reid McIntyre, Mary Annella Frank (steel sculpture), Tazuko Ichikawa, Richard Ford, David Nez, Wolfgang Jasper, Betsy Packard, Taro Ichihashi, Arthur Cadieux, James Brinsfield.

SELECTION OF NEW ARTISTS: Artists may send a letter with slides, resumé, and recommendations, and may submit with the intention of being in a group show rather than a solo show. Shows are scheduled two years in advance. The gallery sponsors new talent shows and an occasional juried show.

ARDEL GALLERIES

1712 21st Street, N.W.
Washington, DC 20009
(202)232-5416
Tuesday, Thursday and Saturday
  12-6 and by appointment

Owner/Director: Elia Ivonne Fuentes
Cash, check, American Express, payment plan
Established 1986

Elia Fuentes is an endodontist, as well as a professor at Georgetown University. She has always been an avid collector of fine art and antiques. This passion led to the establishment of Ardel when her collection began to overflow. A block from the Phillips Collection, the Ardel Galleries occupy the first floor of her magnificent townhouse near Dupont Circle.

Ardel's emphasis is on exposing contemporary art by Latin American artists. Fuentes has worked with the Organization of American States and other organizations to sponsor exhibitions, lectures, and community projects which benefit Latin American artists. However, committed to living in and contributing to Washington, Fuentes has made an equal priority of showing work by area artists.

MEDIA: So far Fuentes has shown paintings and other traditional media, but she is open to showing any medium including video if there is a way to do so.

STYLES: "No emphasis on any particular type of art; more emphasis is given to the artist" and whether the work is consistent, professionally presented and executed, and attractive.

ARTISTS REGULARLY SHOWN: Latin American artists include: Olga Donde, Mexico; Maria Auda, Chile (impressionist paintings in oil, watercolor, pastel); Luis Vargas Saavedra, Chile; Francesco Castilio (realistic oils and watercolors). Washington artists include Julia Byrne (graphite drawings of fields of flowers); Augustin Blasquez (Egyptian-derived three-dimensional reliefs with gold leaf); Virginia Daley (oils and pastels).

SELECTION OF NEW ARTISTS: Artists may send a letter with a resumé and slides. Shows are scheduled six months to one year in advance.

Harbor, 1987, by Frits Goosen. Oil on canvas, 14"x18". Atlantic Gallery.

ATLANTIC GALLERY

1055 Thomas Jefferson Street, N.W.
Washington, DC 20007
(202)337-2299
Monday-Saturday 10-6,
Sunday 1-5

Director: Virginia Smith
Price Range: $100-25,000
Cash, check, MasterCard, Visa,
American Express, payment plan
Established 1975

    The Atlantic Gallery, in the Foundry Mall, is next to the Canal in Georgetown. It is appropriate that this gallery is on the water, as Atlantic specializes in nautical paintings and graphics by British and American artists. Although the work is very traditionally executed, almost all of it has been produced by living contemporary artists. Landscapes, hunting scenes, and cityscapes are also on hand.
    A select stock of 18th and 19th century graphics includes architectural prints; works by Piranesi and other important period artists are also available.
    The gallery publishes a regular newsletter highlighting several of the artists and artworks to be featured in upcoming exhibits. Finally, custom framing services are offered.
    MEDIA: Oil paintings, original prints, watercolors, offset prints of varying edition sizes; historic prints; restrike engravings.
    STYLES: Very traditional.
    ARTISTS REGULARLY SHOWN: Contemporary nautical artists: Robert Back, J. Robert Burnell, Roy Cross (Chesapeake Bay painter), Frits Goosen (Dutch), Alan Maley, John Stobart. Also Herring (hunt scenes).
    SELECTION OF NEW ARTISTS: Artists working in appropriate styles are welcome to send a letter with a resumé and slides.

FRANZ BADER GALLERY

1701 Pennsylvania Avenue, N.W.
Washington, DC 20006
(202)659-5515
Tuesday-Saturday 10-6

Owner/Director: Wretha Hanson
Price Range: $20-20,000
Cash, check, MasterCard, Visa,
American Express, payment plan
Established 1953

A block from the Renwick and two blocks from the White House, the Franz Bader Gallery is in a powerful location. For that matter, it is a powerful gallery—but that power has been earned with integrity and given back to artists with care.

In 1939, Franz Bader and his wife fled Europe and came to Washington. He worked for a bookstore/gallery and eventually became manager of the gallery arm. In 1953 he opened his own gallery, with the intention that no good local artist would ever have to feel as homeless as he had been. He exhibited contemporary art; 75 percent of it was by local artists, a practice unheard of even in New York at the time.

Franz Bader Gallery was bought in 1985 by Wretha Hanson, who shares Bader's concern for Washington artists. Bader, then 81, had lost his lease and decided that he had earned his retirement. Hanson considers herself to be a torch-bearer. The Bader Gallery continues to emphasize new works by Washington area artists.

An interesting feature is the annual show of art by Eskimos.

Low-priced prints are available in the Print Rack.

Finally, custom framing and art consulting services are offered.

This glass-fronted, high-ceilinged gallery is a pleasure to visit for many reasons.

MEDIA: Sculpture, paintings, drawings, prints, ceramic, fine crafts, hand-built furniture.

STYLES: Contemporary and very eclectic; traditional to experimental.

ARTISTS REGULARLY SHOWN: Michael Platt; James Iritani; F. L. Wall; Herman Maril; Otto Natzler; Evan Summer (surrealist paintings and prints, unpeopled urbanscapes); Hilda Thorpe (three-dimensional handmade paper, colorful forms).

SELECTION OF NEW ARTISTS: Artists interested in representation may send a letter with slides and resumé, call for an appointment, or drop in. Three galleries are in operation: painting, sculpture, and prints/works on paper; each hosts a one-person show for three weeks at a time to bring Washington about 50 solo shows per year.

BAUMGARTNER GALLERIES INC.

2016 R Street, N.W.
Washington, DC 20009
(202)232-6320
Tuesday-Sunday 11-6
Member Washington Art Dealers Association,
  Dupont Circle Fine Art Galleries

Owner: Manfred Baumgartner
Directors: Adrian Michaelson and Patricia Crews
Cash, check, MasterCard, Visa, payment plan
Established 1979

Austrian-born Manfred Baumgartner has been in the business of promoting art and artists in the Washington area for some 20 years. He began as a private agent for Friedensreich Hundertwasser, whom he still represents.

Baumgartner continues to emphasize promoting and placing gallery artists in major public and private collections, including museums such as the Hirshhorn, and corporate collections such as GTE. The gallery organizes travelling exhibitions for such spaces.

MEDIA: Paintings and graphic work; also sculpture, assemblages, collage.

STYLES: Usually abstract, including abstract-expressionist, minimalist, and Washington Color School.

ARTISTS REGULARLY SHOWN: Painters: Christian Attersee, the estate of Leon Berkowitz, Hundertwasser, Sherry Zvares Sanabria, Jochen Seidel, Carroll Sockwell, Robin Rose, Mindy Weisel, William Willis. Sculptors: Steven Bickley, Peter Charles, Scott McIntyre, Jesus Bautista Moroles, Beverly Pepper, Jeff Spaulding, James Wolfe.

SELECTION OF NEW ARTISTS: Artists may send a letter with resumé and slides.

SANDRA BERLER, DEALER FINE PHOTOGRAPHIC PRINTS

7002 Connecticut Avenue
Chevy Chase, MD 20815
(301)656-8144
By appointment only
Member Association of International Photography Art Dealers

Owner/Director: Sandra Berler
Cash, check
Established 1984

Sandra Berler, a private dealer, has been handling contemporary and vintage photography since 1976. She now presents the work of internationally known photographers in a gallery connected to her Victorian house.

MEDIA: Black-and-white silver prints and platinum prints, color works, and photogravures.

STYLES: Traditional to surrealist, figurative to conceptual, abstract, expressionistic, and photojournalistic.

ARTISTS REGULARLY SHOWN: Berenice Abbott, Manuel Alvarez Bravo, William Clift, Bruce Davidson, Mitch Epstein, Robert Frank, Koudelka, Helen Levitt, Jerome Liebling, Elaine Mayes, Joel Meyerowitz, and Ingemorath.

SELECTION OF NEW ARTISTS: Artists are welcome to send a letter with slides or photographic prints, resumé, and recommendations.

BIRD-IN-HAND GALLERY AND BOOKSTORE

323 7th Street, S.E.
At Eastern Market
Washington, DC 20003
(202)543-0744
Tuesday-Sunday 11-6

Owner/Director: Christopher Ackerman
Price Range: $50-650
Cash, check, MasterCard, Visa, payment plan
Established 1982 in Richmond,
1987 in Washington

Bird-in-Hand does indeed have two in the bush: artwork and books.

The books are all on art, architecture, and photography. Lots of art exhibition catalogs are available as well. The books are neatly displayed in shelves which are three feet or so high.

Artwork hangs above the bookshelves. Shows change monthly.

MEDIA: Usually small works in the media of original prints and photography; also small paintings, drawings, and sculpture.

STYLES: Generally fairly traditional including representational, with some abstract. Commissions can be arranged.

ARTISTS REGULARLY SHOWN: Washington area emerging professionals, including: Andrea Burchette (ink on paper, representational landscapes); Penelope Mayer (egg tempera and oil paintings); Isabelle Tokumaru; Barbara B. Stephens; Michelle Montalbano; Madge Matteo; Ester Espeto; Allan Scherr (hand-colored nature photos, platinum prints).

SELECTION OF NEW ARTISTS: Ackerman says, "Artists selected will hopefully care to be represented throughout the year, not just during one specified period of exhibition time." Interested artists are invited to send resumé and slides or to telephone for an appointment. New artists are chosen based on proficiency of technique and professionalism.

Bruce in a Decorated Sweater, 1986, by Andrew Hudson. Etching and aquatint, ed. 20, 15"x22^1/2". Photograph by Joel Breger. Brody's Gallery.

BRODY'S GALLERY

1706 21st Street, N.W.
Washington, DC 20009
(202)462-4747
Tuesday-Saturday 11-5:30
Member Washington Art Dealers Association,
  Dupont Circle Fine Art Galleries

Owner/Director: Tom Brody
Cash, check, payment plan
Established 1983

Brody's Gallery, housed in two stories of a Dupont Circle townhouse, fills its space every month except August with strong work by contemporary artists. Tom Brody says, "I like strong, figurative, narrative work with good color, and conceptual art."

The work here is almost always provocative. Potentially controversial work with political, social, and sexual overtones is given equal importance with relatively peaceful work. Brody is generally concerned with good ideas which address issues both current and ongoing.

MEDIA: Paintings, drawings, original prints, sculpture, photography, handmade paper.

STYLES: All contemporary styles short of extremely experimental.

ARTISTS REGULARLY SHOWN: Benita Berman, Mark Clark, Andrew Hudson, Jacqueline Hayden (photographs, some as large as 30"x40"), Rebecca Kamen, Percy Martin, Keith Morrison (large figurative paintings), Sylvia Snowden, Andrea Way.

SELECTION OF NEW ARTISTS: Brody says, "We're pretty full but we're always willing to look." Artists interested in representation may phone for an appointment. New artists are chosen based on originality, content, and proficiency of technique.

ROBERT BROWN CONTEMPORARY ART

1005 New Hampshire Avenue, N.W.
Washington, DC 20037
(202)822-8737
Tuesday-Saturday 11-5 and by appointment

Owner/Director: Robert Brown
Cash, check, payment plan
Established 1980

Robert Brown Contemporary Art occupies three floors of a townhouse. It is a light-filled gallery with an atrium; both the space and the art shown convey a serious, scholarly feeling.

Robert Brown, a lawyer, was a private dealer in Switzerland before he ran his gallery in New York for three years. He handles contemporary art usually by recognized European artists.

MEDIA: Paintings, drawings, original prints, sculpture, photography, collage.

STYLES: All contemporary styles short of extremely experimental.

ARTISTS REGULARLY SHOWN: Hannelore Baron, Oliveira Cezar, Jay Dunitz, Mario Eichmann, Kit-Keung-Kan, Oleg Kudryashov, Richard Niewerth, Picasso's illustrated books, Fifo Stricker, Joseph Solman, Alfredo Halegua, Henry Moore (prints and sculpture), Shahla Arbabi, Hans Sieverding.

SELECTION OF NEW ARTISTS: Artists interested in representation may send a letter with slides and a resumé.

BUFFALO GALLERY

127 South Fairfax Street
Alexandria, VA 22314
(703)548-3338
Tuesday-Saturday 11-5, Sunday 1-5,
and by appointment

Owner/Directors: John and Pam King
Price Range: $50 up
Cash, check, MasterCard, Visa,
payment plan
Established 1984

Tucked away on a quiet street just a few steps from King Street, Buffalo Gallery specializes in American western art and craft work, including native American work. The work here is authentic and fine; a wide variety of styles and media is represented.

A small percentage of the work available at Buffalo is semi-antique, i.e. native American baskets and pottery c. 1900; but the majority of the work is recent work by contemporary native American and western artists.

MEDIA: Paintings; sculpture (wood, terra cotta, limited edition bronzes); photographs; original prints; crafts (Navajo rugs, other textiles, Acoma pottery, jewelry and other wearables).

STYLES: Western. If the work is done by native Americans, the styles are passed-down and traditional.

ARTISTS REGULARLY SHOWN: Retha Walden Gambaro (medicine wheels and limited edition sculpture), Allan Houser (bronzes), Gary Price (waterfowl bronzes), Charles Smith (pressed and carved clay pieces), Eyvind Earle (serigraphs), Mary Ann Ginter (western landscape paintings).

SELECTION OF NEW ARTISTS: If an American Indian, western resident, or western-influenced artist is interested in representation, s/he is welcome to send a letter with slides and a resumé.

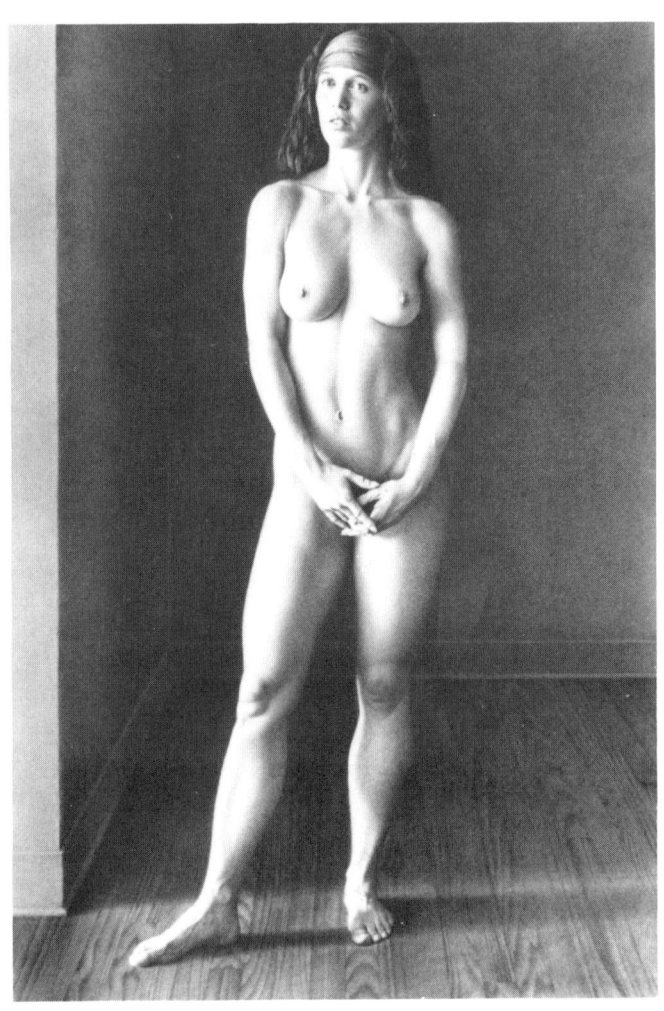

Angela in Morning Light, 1987, by Robert Julius Brawley. Graphite on paper, 48"x33". Capricorn Galleries.

CAPRICORN GALLERIES

4849 Rugby Avenue
Bethesda, MD 20814
(301)657-3477
Tuesday-Friday 10-5 and 7-9;
Saturday 10-6; Sunday 1-5

Owner/Director: Philip Desind
Price Range: $200-50,000
Cash, check, payment plan
Established 1964

Something is always happening at Capricorn. Old friends and clients are constantly dropping in. Even though this huge gallery consists of 2,300 square feet, Philip ("Phil") Desind manages to find so many outstanding pieces of artwork that many are stacked against the walls, underneath the hanging paintings. Visitors are encouraged to browse through these stacks. While you have taken this in, the phone has rung 12 times. Capricorn is a friendly place and it always seems to be open.

Desind's passion for paintings started during the WPA days when he worked in New York as the director of the remedial reading program in the city's high schools. Though he began collecting art around then, he did not open his gallery until 30 years later. In the meantime, Desind did it all. He designed the U.S. Post Office's mail-counting system. A statistician and mathematician, he was a professor at American University. Even now, not content merely to run one of the finest galleries in the area, he is writing a book about American and Canadian wood sculptors.

Desind does not carry any artwork which he would not be willing to buy; in fact, he often does so. He has amassed a major collection of contemporary American realist art. He takes special delight in discovering emerging artists—he has contributed to the comfort if not the stardom of many—and re-championing worthy forgotten artists. For example, Capricorn was one of the first galleries to rediscover Albert Bierstadt. In 1965, one could have purchased a Bierstadt painting at Capricorn for only a few hundred dollars.

MEDIA: Primarily paintings; also drawings, original prints, collage, sculpture.
STYLES: Contemporary realism.
ARTISTS REGULARLY SHOWN: A brief list of represented artists includes: Ernest Albert Land, Dana Winslow, Sharon Wolpoff, Ned Bittinger, Patrick Normyle, Gary Hughes, Susan Murphy, Mary Etta Thorn, Alice Corbett, Ralph Smith. Works by Roger Medearis, Robert Riggs, and others are also available.
SELECTION OF NEW ARTISTS: Artists working in representational styles may send a letter with slides and resumé, or call for an appointment. New artists are chosen based on proficiency of technique, originality, and consistency/professionalism. Shows are scheduled one to two years in advance. Solo shows take up one gallery, and the remaining two are given to changing group shows which Desind curates.

PATRICIA CAREGA GALLERY

3251 Prospect Street, N.W.
Washington, DC 20007
(202)333-2593, -8749
Monday-Friday 10-6,
Saturday 12-6

Owner/Director: Patricia Carega
Price Range: $150-10,000
Cash, check, MasterCard, Visa,
American Express, payment plan
Established 1985

Patricia Carega has lived in Rome, Paris, and Florence. Her international background has led her to show art from around the world as well as contemporary American work. She has a special interest in unique objects—she loves whimsical, humorous pieces, as well as the book-as-art.

Patricia Carega Gallery is a small establishment in the courtyard of Georgetown Court.

MEDIA: Paintings, sculpture (including *objets* and book art).

STYLES: Generally abstract, including expressionist, abstract-expressionist, minimalist, conceptual; some surrealist and naive. Commissions can be arranged.

ARTISTS REGULARLY SHOWN: Philip Jamison (Maine painter of landscapes and interiors), Herbert Creecy, Richard Vogl (German expressionist), Breton Morse, Philippe Labarthe (Paris surrealist), Jacques Soisson, Elizabeth Freize, Stephen Myers (Virginia sculptor), Anita Bucher Godfroy, Mokha Laget (Washington artist; mystical work with charts, maps, numbers).

SELECTION OF NEW ARTISTS: Artists may send a letter with resumé and slides. New artists are selected based on originality, consistency, and proficiency of technique. Shows are scheduled up to two years in advance.

CITY GALLERY

Please refer to the next chapter, Cooperative Galleries.

Untitled, 1987,
by Robert Roesch.
Steel, 44"x47"x14".
Ernst Alexander Gallery.

ERNST ALEXANDER GALLERY

1655 Wisconsin Avenue, N.W.
Washington, DC 20007
(202)338-4510
Tuesday-Saturday 11-6, Sunday 12-5

Owner/Directors: Adriana Ernst
and Virginia Alexander
Cash, check
Established 1987

Proprietors Adriana Ernst and Virginia Alexander have, respectively, a degree in arts management and experience as a local artist. Their intention is to show "the best contemporary art on the scene today" in this new gallery. Ernst is Venezuelan, and many of the artists on the exhibition schedule are South American.

MEDIA: Paintings, sculpture, drawings, original prints, wearables.

STYLES: Most contemporary styles short of experimental.

ARTISTS REGULARLY SHOWN: Lobo (bronze sculpture), Robert Roesch (works of metal), Gandi (wood sculpture), Frank Hyder (paintings on large carved wooden surfaces), Alirio Palacios (paintings), Victor Vasarely (paintings and prints).

SELECTION OF NEW ARTISTS: Artists interested in representation at Ernst Alexander are encouraged to send a letter with slides and a resumé, or phone for an appointment. Shows are scheduled three months to one year in advance.

KATHLEEN EWING GALLERY

1609 Connecticut Avenue, N.W., Suite 200　　Owner/Director: Kathleen Ewing
Washington, DC 20009　　Price Range: $100-10,000
(202)328-0955　　Cash, check, payment plan
Wednesday-Saturday 11-6　　Established 1976
Member Association of International Photography Art Dealers,
　Washington Art Dealers Association,
　Dupont Circle Fine Art Galleries

　　Kathleen Ewing Gallery is unusual. Not only does it specialize in one very specific medium, but the medium—photography—is one of the babies of art media, being only about 150 years old. The gallery is unusual for a second reason: the establishment and success of its second location in New York City at 51 Greene Street, in SoHo. Third, it shares a space with another gallery, Marie Martin Gallery.
　　Along with a large selection of contemporary work, Kathleen Ewing has examples of 19th century photography in good-to-excellent condition both in inventory and in some of her monthly shows. For example, A. Aubrey Bodine, who lived in Baltimore and photographed locally, was one of the few photographers to capture Chesapeake Bay life in the early 20th century, and Bodine's work is available here.
　　MEDIA: Photography. Additionally, rare shows feature artists working in painting, drawing, and graphic media, i.e. the 1984 show of work by Lou and Di Stovall, master printmakers.
　　STYLES: Ewing best likes landscape photography and pictorialist photography; work here is strong yet often atmospheric.
　　ARTISTS REGULARLY SHOWN: A. Aubrey Bodine, Steve Szabo, Mark Power (a photo professor at the Corcoran, as well as an art critic whose writings have appeared in *The Washington Post, Washington Review,* and *New Art Examiner*), Allen Appel (also a novelist; *Time After Time* is to his credit), Frank DiPerna, Claudia Smigrod, Eileen Toumanoff, Allan Janus.
　　SELECTION OF NEW ARTISTS: Artists interested in representation are welcome to phone for an appointment, or send a letter with slides and a resumé. New artists are selected based on originality/content, professionalism of presentation, and consistency in work. Shows are booked six months or more in advance. New talent shows are sponsored.

FENDRICK GALLERY

3059 M Street, N.W.
Washington, DC 20007
(202)338-4500
Monday-Saturday 9:30-5:30
Member Washington Art Dealers Association

Owner/Director: Barbara Fendrick
Cash, check
Established 1960

On the busiest street in the heart of Georgetown, the Fendrick Gallery handles contemporary American work by artists from around the nation.

Barbara Fendrick gave Helen Frankenthaler, Robert Rauschenberg, Louise Nevelson, Jasper Johns, and many other "stars" their first one-person Washington shows. In fact, for some of them she mounted their first one-person shows, period.

Fendrick has always been ahead of her time. 10 years ago she sponsored a show called "The Book as Art." The growth of general appreciation of that particular medium is old news to her. Fendrick enjoys a national reputation for being one of Washington's best dealers of contemporary work.

A Young Collectors' gallery has been christened on the second of the three floors of Fendrick Gallery.

Large slide files are available to architects, designers, and collectors whether corporate, museum, or private.

MEDIA: Paintings, graphics, sculpture, architectural ornamentation, collage, glass, ceramics, furniture-as-art, artists' books.

STYLES: Contemporary art, all styles. Commissions can be arranged.

ARTISTS REGULARLY SHOWN: Albert Paley (architectural metalwork), Walter Dusenbery (stone and iron sculpture), Robert Birmelin, Robert Arneson, Patricia T. Forrester, Wendell Castle (furniture), Sam Gilliam (Washington Color School painter), Robin Rose, Barton Benes, Tom Patti.

SELECTION OF NEW ARTISTS: Artists interested in representation may send a letter with slides and a resumé. This gallery actively solicits commissions for its painters and sculptors both locally and nationally.

FISHER GALLERIES

1511 Connecticut Avenue, N.W.
Washington, DC 20036
(202)265-6255
Tuesday-Saturday 10-6

Owner/Director: Miriam Fisher Reno
Cash, check, MasterCard, Visa,
American Express, payment plan
Established 1960

A block north of Dupont Circle, Fisher Galleries is in a ground floor storefront space. The main floor of Fisher Galleries features contemporary American impressionist oil paintings and a select group of realist bronze sculptures. The downstairs gallery shows Chinese antiquities.

MEDIA: Paintings, sculpture.

STYLES: Contemporary impressionist and realist.

ARTISTS REGULARLY SHOWN: Impressionist oil painters: Oppenheim, Gisson, Lentz, Frazier, Warik. Realist oil painters: Heath, Caswell, Brulé. Watercolorist: Beverly Buan.

SELECTION OF NEW ARTISTS: The gallery is not currently interested in representing additional artists.

FOUNDRY GALLERY

Please refer to the next chapter, Cooperative Galleries.

FOXHALL GALLERY

3301 New Mexico Avenue, N.W.
Washington, DC 20016
(202)966-7144
Monday-Saturday 10-5

Directors: Jerry Eisley and Caryl Brody
Cash, check, MasterCard, Visa,
payment plan
Established 1976

Foxhall Gallery, in Foxhall Square, is in upper Northwest near American University. Founded by Jerry Eisley in 1976, the gallery has steadily grown and now represents 20 to 30 artists. Caryl Brody, formerly of the late Hallway Gallery, joined in 1985 as associate director. The collaboration has been productive; Foxhall is showing some exciting, well-crafted work.

MEDIA: Paintings, drawings, sculpture, collage, original prints.

STYLES: Representational, impressionist, expressionist, naive, abstract, abstract expressionist. Commissions can be arranged.

ARTISTS REGULARLY SHOWN: Dean Larson (realist paintings including portraits); Evelyn Turner; Ed Larsen (folk art wind toys, some politically oriented); George Wingate *(a la prima* oil paintings); John Olson (fanciful, quirky bird sculptures of painted metal); James Jones (watercolors); Nick Paciorek (oils, cityscapes); David Zuccarini (realist paintings).

SELECTION OF NEW ARTISTS: Artists interested in representation may phone for an appointment, or send slides and resumé. New artists are selected based on proficiency of technique, originality of vision, and consistency in work. Shows are booked a year in advance.

Untitled, 1987, by Robert Hite. Oil on canvas, 57 1/2"x74".
Foxley/Leach Gallery.

FOXLEY/LEACH GALLERY

3214 O Street, N.W.
Washington, DC 20007
(202)337-3661
Tuesday-Saturday 11-5 and by appointment

Owners: James and Elisabeth Leach
Director: Elisabeth Foxley Leach
Cash, check, payment plan
Established 1986

The Foxley/Leach Gallery is housed in a classic Georgetown two-story townhouse. However, its large terraced sculpture garden is a very unusual feature of either a Washington townhouse or gallery. The gallery frequently features solo shows of outdoor sculpture in this garden.

James Leach is a Congressman (R. Iowa). In spite of leading the busy life of a Congressman's wife, Elisabeth Foxley Leach has managed to channel her passion for art collecting into the care and feeding of a successful gallery. She is handling contemporary American art. Not surprisingly, she is very interested in exposing the work of Midwestern artists to the Washington audience. Work exhibited at Foxley/Leach often is either suitable for architectural installation, or seems to have a statuesque, architectural quality of its own even if it is a wall piece—Leach is an architectural historian.

MEDIA: Paintings, sculpture, works on paper, original prints, signed offsets, photography, architectural, collage.

STYLES: Generally abstract, including expressionist, abstract-expressionist. Also contemporary impressionist and architectural work.

ARTISTS REGULARLY SHOWN: Painters: Robert Bauer, Tom Dineen, Robert Hite, Stephen Moore. Sculptors: David Hubbard, Dan Murray, Duncan Tebow, Janos Enyedi. Artists from around the U.S. are shown; the Leaches like to feature Washington area artists too. They take delight in exposing new talent.

SELECTION OF NEW ARTISTS: Artists may send a letter with resumé and slides; also, open jury days are Wednesdays and Fridays. New artists are chosen based on originality, proficiency of technique, show experience, and sales record. Shows are scheduled about a year in advance. New talent and other group shows are mounted.

La Tete Voilée, 1950,
by Henri Matisse.
Lithograph, $10^3/4" \times 7^5/8"$.
Galerie Lareuse.

GALERIE LAREUSE

2820 Pennsylvania Avenue, N.W.
Washington, DC 20007
(202)333-5704
11-6 Monday-Saturday,
  12-5 Sunday

Owner: J. Michel Lareuse
Director: Royce Burton
Price Range: $100-50,000
Cash, check, MasterCard, Visa,
American Express, payment plan
Established 1983

    J. Michel Lareuse established Galerie Lareuse when the family art collection got out of hand. The gallery, housed in a century-old two-story rowhouse in Georgetown, specializes in artwork of the French School; the walls are covered with prints. Select American prints made before 1940 are available. Authenticity is guaranteed.
    Along with the graphics of historical interest are paintings and drawings by contemporary artists working in French styles.
    The gallery often accepts pieces on consignment and is also known to buy outright select pieces.
    MEDIA: Paintings, drawings, sculpture, prints.
    STYLES: Representational, impressionist, surrealist, abstract.
    ARTISTS REGULARLY SHOWN: Jean Lareuse (paintings and lithographs), Tony Marrinan (pastels). Also, graphics by Braque, Calder, Cassatt, Chagall, Dufy, Leger, Miro, Matisse, Picasso, Renoir, Rouault, Toulouse-Lautrec, Whistler, and many others.
    SELECTION OF NEW ARTISTS: Artists interested in representation may call for an appointment. Accepted artists "share common values with mainly French masters of 20th century art."

GALERIE TRIANGLE

3701 14th Street, N.W.
Washington, DC 20010
(202)829-2323
Tuesday-Saturday 2-6

Owner/Directors: Averille and Charles Jacobs
Price Range: $10-4,000
Cash, check, American Express, art rental,
lease/purchase plan, payment plan
Established 1978

Averille and Charles Jacobs are very committed to giving talented local and national artists and a variety of styles a forum. Emerging artists are especially encouraged to apply. Solo and group shows are mounted.

Beginning collectors are encouraged here, too. Triangle offers a variety of ways to enjoy the presence of art, including lease/purchase, approval, and layaway plans.

But this gallery is not just for the beginning collector. Galerie Triangle gets frequent critical recognition, in *The Washington Post* and elsewhere.

MEDIA: Small works including paintings, drawings, original prints, artists' books/paper, photography, sculpture, collage, crafts, wearables.

STYLES: The gallery does not specialize at this time.

ARTISTS REGULARLY SHOWN: Although the gallery does not have a permanent "stable" of represented artists, a large number of artists are exhibited regularly, including: W. E. Neudorfer, Russell H. Everett, Jacqueline Lee, Christine Girvan, Sherman Edwards, Augustin Blazquez, Vel Marshall.

SELECTION OF NEW ARTISTS: Artists may send, or drop in with, slides and a resumé; or they may phone for an appointment. Frequent juried shows are sponsored.

GALLERY 4

115 S. Columbus Street
Alexandria, VA 22314
(703)548-4600
Tuesday-Saturday 10-5

Partners: Lynne Dearborn, Lee
King, Mary Kay Ryan
Price Range: $200-8,000
Cash, check, MasterCard, Visa, payment plan
Established 1974

Mounting seven interesting shows of contemporary artwork each year, Gallery 4 promotes area artists working in most media.

Gallery 4 also offers an art consulting division which can locate art for corporate clients in the area. Custom framing services are available.

MEDIA: Paintings, drawings, sculpture, photography, original prints.

STYLES: Representational, expressionist, abstract-expressionist, experimental, conceptual, Washington Color School.

ARTISTS REGULARLY SHOWN: More than 35, including: Deborah Ellis (watercolors and prints), William Dunlap (oils), Carrita Smith (oils), Rosaline Moore (oils), John Morrell (gouache), Ellen Glasgow (oils), Ann Slaughter (mixed media on canvas).

SELECTION OF NEW ARTISTS: Interested artists may send a letter with slides and resumé or call for an appointment. New artists are chosen based primarily on consistency and originality. Shows are scheduled one to two years in advance.

GALLERY 10

Please refer to the next chapter, Cooperative Galleries.

A Past Within #7, 1987, by Lisa Brotman. Acrylic and oil on paper, 40"x60". Gallery K.

GALLERY K

2010 R Street, N.W.
Washington, DC 20009
(202)234-0339
Tuesday-Saturday 11-6
Member Washington Art Dealers Association,
  Dupont Circle Fine Art Galleries

Owners: H. Marc Moyens, Komei Wachi
Director: Komei Wachi
Price Range: $300 up
Cash, check, payment plan
Established 1975

Gallery K moved in November 1986 to a huge new space. K's 2,000 sq. ft. of skylit space takes up two floors of a beautifully designed townhouse near Dupont Circle.

Gallery K has become well-known as a place where well-crafted work with surrealist overtones is shown. What is perhaps less apparent is that Marc Moyens and Komei Wachi take special delight in exposing young, very talented, but previously unknown artists from around the world. If they can act as matchmakers with young and unknown collectors, all the better.

Some of their legendary "bargain basement" events have made news not only because of the quality of the work available, but also because the lines of people waiting for the gallery to open went around the block.

MEDIA: Paintings, drawings, sculpture, collage, original prints, installations, ceramic.

STYLES: Surrealist, figurative, realist, abstract, naive, American Indian, folk, primitive.

ARTISTS REGULARLY SHOWN: Susan Abbott, Edwin Ahlstrom, François Dillasser, Fred Folsom (Washington realist painter), Lani Irwin (surrealist painter, mannequin themes), Judy Jashinsky, Jody Mussoff (colored pencil drawings), Wayne Paige, Jo Rango, Eve Watts (ceramic figurative works), David Wolfe, Lisa Brotman (a professor at the Corcoran).

SELECTION OF NEW ARTISTS: Artists interested in representation may send slides and a resumé or drop in with same. New artists are selected based on originality of content and consistency in work. Shows are booked 18 months in advance.

GALLERY WEST

Please refer to the next chapter, Cooperative Galleries.

GILPIN GALLERY

1 Prince Street
Alexandria, VA 22314
(703)836-0110
Tuesday-Saturday 10-5, Sunday 1-5

Owners: Helen Nelson, Maryanne Kowalesky
Director: Maryanne Kowalesky
Price Range: $600-10,000
Cash, check, MasterCard, Visa,
American Express, payment plan
Established 1982

In an especially lovely building and block of Old Town Alexandria, Gilpin Gallery is just 100 yards from the Potomac waterfront. A variety of work including one-of-a-kind and multiples is available.

MEDIA: Paintings, drawings, wearables, prints (originals, and medium to large edition offsets), sculpture (original and limited edition).

STYLES: Representational, impressionist, expressionist, abstract.

ARTISTS REGULARLY SHOWN: Caroline Huff, Pil Ju Templeton, Catherine Frisch, Bernard Frigara, Harrison Mangan, Donald Zolan, Enzo Cini, Jiang, Dennis Patrick Lewan.

SELECTION OF NEW ARTISTS: Artists interested in representation may phone for an appointment.

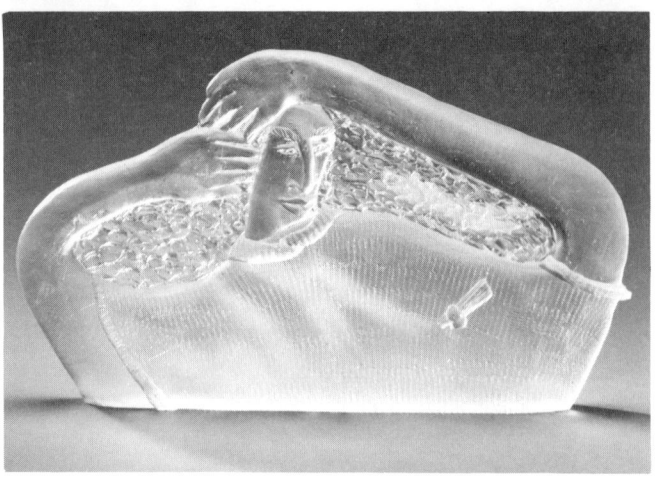

Listening Hunter, by Stephen Dale Edwards. Cast and sandblasted glass, 12"x18^{1}/4"x4". Photograph by Robert Vinnedge. Glass Gallery.

GLASS GALLERY

4931 Elm Street
Bethesda, MD 20814
(301)657-3478
Tuesday-Saturday 11-5

Owner/Director: Sarah Eveleth Hansen
Price Range: Up to $10,000
Cash, check, MasterCard, Visa, payment plan
Established 1973

Sarah Hansen started out as an antiques dealer. She became interested in antique glass, and her interest and research led her to contemporary glass. First she operated a glass gallery in the back room of her antique shop; but for the last seven years, she has been dealing exclusively in contemporary glass in "a wide range of styles and approaches using glass as an art rather than a craft medium." Work here is generally colorful and luminous.

She has been working with some high-powered artists. Several of them have shown at the Corning Museum of Glass as well as the Renwick Gallery.

The Glass Gallery is between Wisconsin Avenue and Arlington Road in Bethesda.

MEDIA: Glass.

STYLES: Primarily sculptural but a few pieces are functional. Commissions can be arranged. Whether conservative or highly abstract, the work here is invariably well-crafted and striking.

ARTISTS REGULARLY SHOWN: About 50 artists are shown in a given year, including: Stephen Dale Edwards (figural cast glass sculpture); Tom McGlauchlin (abstract mixed media sculpture); Kent Ipsen (large cast glass sculpture); Patrick Wadley (sandblasted imagery on blown pieces); John Nickerson (fabricated glass sculpture and blown glass vessels); Richard LaLonds (fused glass panels and vessels); Ruth Brockmann (fused glass masks); Douglas Anderson (*paté de verre* nature pieces); Benjamin Moore (blown glass bowls and lamps); Richard Royal (blown vessels).

SELECTION OF NEW ARTISTS: Artists may send a letter with slides, resumé, and recommendations, or phone for an appointment. New artists are chosen based on originality of content, consistency, and proficiency of technique. Shows are scheduled six months or more in advance.

Sam Shepard, 1985,
by Annie Liebowitz.
Silver print photograph,
24"x20".
Govinda Gallery.

GOVINDA GALLERY

1227 34th Street, N.W.
Washington, DC 20007
(202)333-1180
Tuesday-Saturday 11-5
Member Washington Art Dealers Association

Owner/Director: Christopher Murray
Price Range: $500-25,000
Cash, check, payment plan
Established 1975

Govinda Gallery, in a small building on the quiet end of Georgetown, deals in contemporary photographs, paintings and drawings. One interesting aspect to this gallery is its interest in book illustration by contemporary artists.

Very strong in its photographic department, Govinda Gallery has on hand the work of several famous photographers. Washington area photographers are also well-represented.

Work shown here is often visionary, imaginative, and spiritual. Whatever the approach, the work favored by Christopher Murray is well-executed, with depth, insight, originality, and punch.

An occasional show offers a different kind of glimpse into the esoteric. For example, the gallery mounted a show in 1986 featuring antiquities from Nepal and Tibet, including antique vases, bowls, and other objects rarely seen outside of that area. The pieces were from the collection of Ian Alsop, a Washington native who had lived in Nepal for 15 years.

MEDIA: Paintings, photographs, works on paper.

STYLES: Representational, surrealist, pop.

ARTISTS REGULARLY SHOWN: About 20 artists are shown in a given year, including Howard Carr (Washington landscape painter), Annie Leibovitz (photographer of stars), Christopher Makos (photographs dealing with architecture and design), Kim Murray, Byron Peck, Mati Klarwein, Ron Wood, "Doc" Edgerton, Matthew Ralston, Erica Leonard, Andy Warhol.

SELECTION OF NEW ARTISTS: Artists may send a letter with slides and recommendations, or phone for an appointment. New artists are chosen based on originality of content and proficiency of technique. Shows are scheduled more than one year in advance.

JANE HASLEM GALLERY (Two locations)

406 7th Street, N.W.	2025 Hillyer Place, N.W.
Washington, DC 20004	Washington, DC 20009
(202)638-6162	(202)638-6162
Wednesday-Saturday 12-5	Friday-Saturday 11-5
and by appointment	and by appointment
Established 1960	Established 1987
Member Washington Art Dealers Association	Owner: Jane Haslem
Cash, check, payment plans	Director: Jeffrey Haslem

Jane Haslem started out as an artist herself. Paying her dues—and the rent—as a studio occupant, she eventually became manager of the studio building as well as of the gallery in which the resident artists showed their work.

Having spent 30 years dealing art, Haslem's reputation is based on her knowledge and collection of prints made by American artists since World War II. She has focused on those printmakers who have contributed to the advancement and innovation of printmaking techniques, and the students who followed them. But not dwelling completely on this specialty, she devotes most of the gallery to excellent contemporary American art of many styles in primarily two-dimensional media.

Jeffrey Haslem's special interest and expertise is original cartoon and comic strip drawings. One can regularly find a large selection of original cartoon drawings by living syndicated cartoonists. Once in awhile the gallery will come up with a surprise show of cartoonists' "serious" artwork in other media.

A nice feature of Haslem Gallery is the printed matter originating there in the forms of informative catalogs and the colorful quarterly newsletter.

MEDIA: Original prints, paintings, drawings; also, original cartoon drawings by syndicated cartoonists.

STYLES: The gamut from abstract, abstract-expressionist, Op/Pop, to loosely-drawn or meticulously-rendered representational works.

ARTISTS REGULARLY SHOWN: The work of over 125 artists can be found at Haslem's, including Leonard Baskin, Billy Morrow Jackson ("photorealistic" paintings, actually painted from memories), Julian Stanczak, Mark Tobey, Richard Ziemann, Leonardo Lasansky, Hayes Friedman (often humorous paintings poking fun at art history), Scip Barnhart, Will Barnet, Michael Mazur. Cartoonists include Garry Trudeau, Jules Feiffer, Pat Oliphant, Tony Auth, Mike Peters, Bill Mauldin.

SELECTION OF NEW ARTISTS: Artists may send slides with a cover letter, and they may submit with the intention of being in a group show rather than a solo show. Artists are chosen based primarily on originality/content, proficiency of technique, and consistency in work. Shows are scheduled two years in advance.

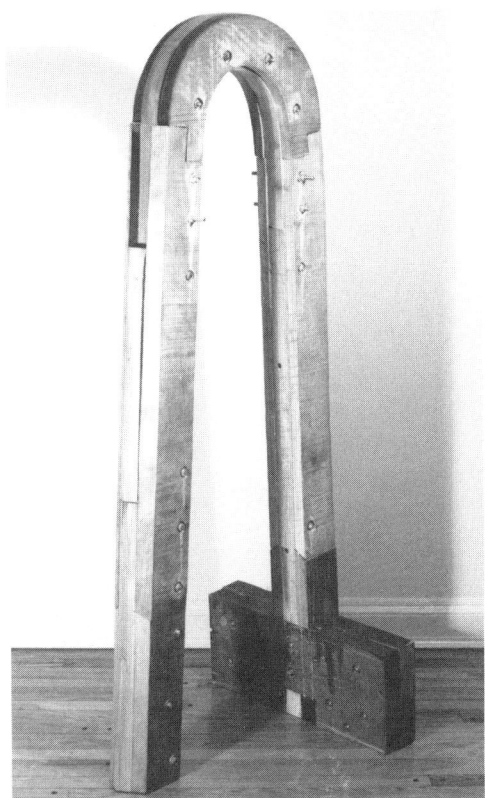

Bent Keel, 1987,
by Douglas Hoagg.
Wood and metal, 65"x24"x27".
Collection of Marsha and
Vohn Bachner.
Henri Gallery.

HENRI GALLERY

1500 21st Street, N.W.
Washington, DC 20036
(202)659-9313
Tuesday-Saturday 11-6, Sunday 2-6
Member Dupont Circle Fine Art Galleries

Owner/Director: Henrietta "Henri" Ehrsam
Cash, check
Established 1958 in Virginia,
1967 in Washington

"Henri" always says "Not Boring" in her gallery advertisements. The work Henri shows is certainly not boring; she has always had a penchant for the highly abstract. She continues to show new work by artists from around the world.
MEDIA: Primarily paintings and sculpture.
STYLES: Abstract, conceptual; all scales.
ARTISTS REGULARLY SHOWN: Painters: Traute Paustian-Ishida, Jean Russo, Paul DeLong, Jacqueline Freedman, Frank Herrmann, Kevin Mullins, Gerald Mitchell, Adell Westbrook, Dave Moreland. Sculptors: Harold Van Houten (stone and steel), Arthur Weyhe, Douglas Hoagg (wood and metals), Lester Van Winkle (wood, bronze, steel), Alan Neider, Dennis Nick, Dennis Harrington, Michael Bigger, Jjon Glidden, Wilhelm Bronner, Don Grant, Italo Scanga, Harry Anderson, Stuart Fink, Rebecca Stephens di Domenico, Brenda Brown, Michael Loomis, William Willers, Tom Williams.
SELECTION OF NEW ARTISTS: Henri generally prefers to discover her artists, but slide/resumé submissions are welcome nonetheless.

Carousel Horses, 1987, by Sid Willis. Oil on canvas, 34"x40". Photograph by Mark Steven Walker. Heritage Gallery of Classical Realism.

HERITAGE GALLERY OF CLASSICAL REALISM

228 South Washington Street
Alexandria, VA 22314
(703)683-5825
Tuesday-Saturday 10-6, Sunday 12-5

Directors: Mark Walker, John Wiegand, Robert DeVaux
Price Range: $1,000-30,000
Cash, check, MasterCard, Visa, American Express, payment plan
Established 1985

    The Heritage Gallery of Classical Realism is a huge enterprise which occupies several rooms covering over 2,000 square feet. The elegantly appointed galleries have been dedicated to a passionate commitment to classical realism. The directors believe in the *atelier* system of training in the craft of painting, so strongly that according to their brochure they "endeavor to secure patronage for the artist" as well as for the *atelier*. The *atelier* course requires years of commitment to drawing from the cast and the figure, and the study of anatomy, still life, landscape painting—Classical Realism.

    A videotape available for viewing at the gallery shows some of the artists at work and explains the gallery directors' philosophy of classical realism.

    Heritage Gallery produces some beautiful printed matter including exhibition catalogs.

    MEDIA: Contemporary paintings, drawings, sculpture.

    STYLES: Very traditional styles by contemporary artists, including representational and impressionist. Commissions, including portraits, can be arranged.

    ARTISTS REGULARLY SHOWN: Over 35 artists are represented, including: Richard Lack (highly colored still life, landscape, portrait, genre, and allegorical paintings); Don Koestner (poetic landscapes); Sid Willis (Boston School painter); Stephen Gjertson; Robert Douglas Hunter; Lisa Bormann; Anna Van Demark; Robert Moore; Peg Yarbrough.

    SELECTION OF NEW ARTISTS: Interested artists may send a letter with slides and a resumé. New artists are chosen for representation based primarily on proficiency of technique, consistency, and professionalism, as well as saleability. Shows are scheduled six months to one year in advance. Artists are welcome to submit slides for consideration for group shows as well as solo shows.

Venice, by Joanna Zjawinska. Serigraph, 27"x36". Inner-Visions, Inc.

INNER-VISIONS OF GEORGETOWN

1055 Thomas Jefferson Street, N.W.
Washington, DC 20007
(202)342-6695; (703)978-8337
Monday-Friday 10-6 (Thursday 10-9) and Sunday 11-4

Owners: Frederic and Carol Ott
Director: Frederic Ott
Price Range: $100-10,000
Cash, check, MasterCard, Visa, American Express, payment plan
Established 1972 in Colorado, 1981 in Virginia, 1987 in Washington

Inner-Vision's main gallery is in the Foundry Building in Georgetown. Their Annandale location, reachable at the second telephone number above, is open by appointment.

Frederic and Carol Ott have been art consultants in the area for years, and they continue to offer consulting services to the design trade, both residential and corporate. But they were handling so much good work, they felt they needed to open a gallery, as their inventory was taking over.

Inner-Visions also houses a custom framing facility.

MEDIA: Paintings, drawings, sculpture including metal wall relief, original prints.

STYLES: Representational, impressionist, abstract, expressionist, abstract-expressionist. Commissions can be arranged.

ARTISTS REGULARLY SHOWN: Artists represented include: Robin Morris, Steve Sholinsky, Bruce Bleach, Joanna Zjawinska, Dan Lencioni, Michael Pease, Tomoe Yokoi, Kyu-Baik Hwang.

SELECTION OF NEW ARTISTS: Artists may send a letter with slides and resumé, or phone for an appointment. New artists are chosen based on originality, consistency, and proficiency of technique.

JONES TROYER

1614 20th Street, N.W.
Washington, DC 20009
(202)328-7189
Wednesday-Saturday 11-5
Member Washington Art Dealers Association

Owners: Katherine Jones and Sally Troyer
Cash, check, payment plan
Established 1984

Jones Troyer is located in an English basement near Dupont Circle. This gallery works with vintage to contemporary photography, as well as contemporary works on paper.

Both Katherine Jones and Sally Troyer are photographers themselves. Of all the photographically oriented galleries in town, Jones Troyer is most likely to show the most avant garde photography. The work shown here generally relates to aesthetic issues.

MEDIA: Photographs, works on paper (drawings, prints). Occasionally videos and paintings.

STYLES: Traditional, conceptual, experimental.

ARTISTS REGULARLY SHOWN: About 25 artists, including John Gossage (contemporary landscapes done in classic black-and-white style), John McIntosh (large color works), Jock Reynolds, Suzanne Hellmuth, Ruth Thorne-Thomsen, Barbara Crane, Zeke Berman, John Pfahl, Dick Drentz (large platinum-palladium landscapes), Mark Cohen (portraits of people on the street). Also Claudia DeMonte (whimsical acrylic paintings and sculpture).

SELECTION OF NEW ARTISTS: Artists may send a letter with slides and a resumé, or may phone for an appointment. New artists are chosen based on originality of content and consistency.

Balanced, 1986, by Antonia Castellanos. Bronze, 20 1/2" in height.
Kimberly Gallery.

KIMBERLY GALLERY OF ART

2445 M Street, N.W.
Washington, DC 20037
(202)223-6346
Monday-Saturday 10-6

Owner/Director: Elena Kimberly
Price Range: $300-100,000
Cash, check
Established 1987

Located within the Westin Hotel, the Kimberly Gallery of Art specializes in the work of Latin American, Portuguese, and Spanish artists. The work shown in this new gallery has been abstract or figurative for the most part.

MEDIA: Paintings, sculpture, works on paper, original prints, collage.

STYLES: Generally abstract including expressionist, conceptual, abstract-expressionist. Some representational work.

ARTISTS REGULARLY SHOWN: The work of 18 artists of primarily Mexican or other Latin extraction is available here, including José Luis Cuevas (dreamlike drawings, psychological overtones), Bunther Gerzso (abstract geometric oil paintings), Cordelia Urueta (abstract oil paintings), Joy Laville (figurative acrylics and pastels), Soriano, Victor Chab (collage with oils), Carulla, Estopiñian (sculpture).

SELECTION OF NEW ARTISTS: Artists of the appropriate ethnic origin may send a letter with slides, resumé, and recommendations.

Untitled, 1986, by John Ferguson. Cor-ten steel, 96" in height. B. R. Kornblatt Gallery.

B. R. KORNBLATT GALLERY
[See Color Plates after page 64]

406 7th Street, N.W.
Washington, DC 20004
(202)638-7657
Tuesday-Saturday 10:30-5:30
Member Washington Art Dealers Association

Owner: Barbara R. Kornblatt
Director: Alan Fisher
Price Range: $1,000 up
Cash, check, payment plan
Established 1975 in Baltimore, 1980 in Washington

B. R. Kornblatt Gallery is on the first floor of The 406. The gallery itself is like one of the clean-cut abstract constructions which would be shown here. The gallery is spacious with high ceilings, so large, bold, brightly colored pieces crop up frequently. Strong contemporary work is the norm.

Both Barbara Kornblatt and Alan Fisher have been professional artists. They are now quite happy to promote art rather than practice it for a living, and they do so passionately. For them, this includes participation in the Chicago International Art Exposition each year, as well as advertising in *Art in America* and other magazines.

MEDIA: Paintings, sculpture including site-specific work, works on paper, original prints, signed offsets, installations, photography, architectural, collage, constructions.

STYLES: Generally abstract, including experimental, minimalist, conceptual, Washington Color School, architectural; also, contemporary impressionist painters.

ARTISTS REGULARLY SHOWN: The work of 25 artists—usually American but sometimes European—can be found at Kornblatt, including Wolf Kahn (American impressionist landscape painter/pastellist), Kenneth Noland (Washington Color School), Willem de Looper (Washington painter), Michael Todd (fabricated metal sculptures), Susan Crowder, Roger Laux Nelson, Agnes Jacobs (colorful relief wall constructions), John Ferguson (welded steel and brass). Artists also shown include Richard Estes, Helen Frankenthaler, David Hockney, Sol LeWitt, Robert Motherwell, Larry Rivers.

SELECTION OF NEW ARTISTS: Artists may send a letter with resumé and slides; new artists are chosen with regard to originality, proficiency of technique, and show experience. Shows are scheduled one year in advance.

MAURINE LITTLETON GALLERY

3822 N Street, N.W.
Washington, DC 20007
(202)333-9307
Tuesday-Saturday 12-6
Member Glass Art Society

Director: Maurine Littleton
Price Range: $500-20,000
Cash, check, MasterCard, Visa,
American Express, payment plan
Established 1984

This gallery handles contemporary American glass and ceramics. Most of the gallery artists approach their media experimentally, imaginatively building colorful wall or pedestal pieces. They work with an eye toward making beautiful, long-lasting artworks out of materials which have heretofore usually been turned into receptacles, windows, paperweights. The results are often stunning, "Why-didn't-I-think-of-that" works. But the functional pieces are just as carefully and well done—they are *objets d'art* on the same level, only useful as well as beautiful.

MEDIA: Contemporary American studio glass and ceramics.

STYLES: Generally very colorful, abstract, well-executed glass and ceramic forms; wall and sculptural pieces including functional pieces.

ARTISTS REGULARLY SHOWN: The work of 75 artists is available, including: Erwin Eisch (blown glass with enamels and/or engraving); James Tanner (ceramic wall pieces with multiple layers of glazes); Harvey K. Littleton (layered blown glass sculptures); Dale Chihuly (blown glass); Joel P. Myers; Kyohei Fujita; Paul Soldner (ceramic pedestal and wall pieces, slab built or thrown and altered); Don Reitz.

SELECTION OF NEW ARTISTS: New artists are interviewed only with a personal introduction/recommendation from someone familiar to the directors.

MARTIN GALLERY

1609 Connecticut Avenue, N.W.
Washington, DC 20009
(202)232-1995
Wednesday-Saturday 11-6
Member Association of International Photography Art Dealers

Owner/Director: Marie Martin
Price Range: $100-20,000
Cash, check, payment plan
Established 1983

The Martin Gallery shares a space with the Kathleen Ewing Gallery. They also share the same specialty, photography.

Marie Martin has on hand a large selection of mostly 20th century photography, but only because proportionally there has been more photography done in the 20th century. She represents some outstanding photographers who live in Washington, as well as artists from around the country and Britain and Scotland.

Of the photography galleries in the area, Martin is the most apt to show photojournalistic work.

MEDIA: Photographs. Silver prints, cibachrome, some experimental.

STYLES: Photojournalistic, landscapes, some abstract.

ARTISTS REGULARLY SHOWN: William Abranowicz, Ansel Adams, Lucien Aigner, Debbie Fleming Caffrey, Robert Epstein, Arthur Grace, Carol Harrison, Francis Benjamin-Johnston, Sally Mann, Joyce Tenneson.

SELECTION OF NEW ARTISTS: Artists interested in representation are welcome to send a letter with slides and a resumé. New artists are selected based on originality/content, consistency in work, and proficiency of technique. Shows are booked a year or more in advance. New talent shows are sponsored.

MARSHA MATEYKA GALLERY

2012 R Street, N.W.
Washington, DC 20009
(202)328-0088
Wednesday-Saturday 11-5 and by appointment
Member Washington Art Dealers Association,
  Dupont Circle Fine Art Galleries

Owner/Director: Marsha Perry Mateyka
Price Range: "Wide"
Cash, check, payment plan
Established 1984

    This gallery is on the first floor of an 1886 townhouse near Dupont Circle. Architectural details like the structure's original, beautifully ornate woodwork, contradict the artwork—but only in period of origin. The overall effect is very interesting and attractive. The artwork shown is generally strong and somewhat abstract.

    Marsha Mateyka's training is in art history. She shows contemporary art by American and European artists, emerging and established.

    MEDIA: Paintings, works on paper, collage, original prints, sculpture, constructions.

    STYLES: A variety of styles; usually on the abstract side.

    ARTISTS REGULARLY SHOWN: Mary Frank (monotypes); Howard Hodgkin (prints); Alex Katz (prints); Robert Motherwell (works on paper); Miklos Pogany (paintings, drawings, monotypes); Aline Feldman (woodcut prints); William T. Wiley (prints and monotypes); Willy Van Sompel (paintings); Nancy Wolf (drawings); Judy Bass (paintings) and Madeleine Keesing (paintings).

    SELECTION OF NEW ARTISTS: Artists may send a letter with slides, a resumé, and recommendations. If the artist interested in representation lives outside the D.C. area s/he must be represented by a gallery in his/her hometown. New artists are chosen based on originality of content, consistency, and education. Shows are scheduled about one year in advance.

MCINTOSH/DRYSDALE GALLERY

406 7th Street, N.W.
Washington, DC 20004
(202)783-5190
Tuesday-Saturday 11-5
Member Washington Art Dealers Association

Owner/Director: Nancy A. Drysdale
Cash, check, payment plan
Established 1977

In The 406, McIntosh/Drysdale is a spacious, lofted gallery on the third floor next to the David Adamson Gallery. Originally known as the Protech Gallery and then the Protech/McIntosh Gallery, it was founded by Max Protech, who moved to New York in 1976. The current owner/director, Nancy Drysdale, came to Washington from Cincinnati where she was also an art dealer.

By whatever name, the McIntosh/Drysdale Gallery has always dealt in strong leading-edge contemporary work both by major and lesser-known artists from America and Europe.

MEDIA: Sculpture, paintings, works on paper, original prints, constructions.

STYLES: Experimental, abstract, minimalist, architectural, conceptual. Commissions can be arranged.

ARTISTS REGULARLY SHOWN: 30-50 artists are shown in a given year. Internationally known artists represented include Alice Aycock (constructions and architectural installations) and William Wegman (photographs featuring his late dog Man Ray and his current "best friend"), as well as Jerry Clapsaddle (Washington area artist and professor of art who produces acrylic stroke paintings based on a grid background), Scott Burton (functional sculpture), Isaac Whitkin (bronzes), and Richard Fleischner (landscape/architectural sculpture).

SELECTION OF NEW ARTISTS: Artists interested in representation may send a letter with slides. Shows are scheduled two years in advance.

MICKELSON GALLERY

707 G Street, N.W.
Washington, DC 20001
(202)628-1734
Monday-Friday 9:30-5,
Saturday 9:30-3
Member Washington Art Dealers Association

Owner/Director: Sidney S. Mickelson
Associate Director: Katrin C. Haley
Price Range: $150-50,000
Cash, check, MasterCard, Visa,
American Express, payment plan
Established 1960

The Mickelson Gallery is across the street from the National Museum of American Art. The door opens into a busy museum-quality framing business. Several antique and semi-antique paintings are displayed above the frame mouldings, along with antique *objets* scattered about for sale.

The gallery next to the framing facility is relatively hushed. With tile floor, quiet lighting, and seating, this area is comfortable. Sidney Mickelson's emphasis is on contemporary realism; the monthly shows provide shifting views of different approaches to representational artwork.

Mickelson also serves as a consultant to corporations and private clients assembling or adding to their collections.

MEDIA: Paintings, sculpture, works on paper, original prints.

STYLES: Realistic work in many modes: traditional realism, surrealism, graphic work, impressionist, and forays into naive and Western styles.

ARTISTS REGULARLY SHOWN: The work of about 50 artists can be found at the Gallery, including M. C. Escher, George Bellows, Fairfield Porter, Frank Wright (Washington realist painter), Norman Ackroyd (one of the foremost contemporary British aquatint etchers who works both in color and black-and-white), Florence Putterman (a Pennsylvania artist who depicts her area in monotypes), Anne Shreve (a West Virginia landscape painter), and John Loeper (primitive paintings).

SELECTION OF NEW ARTISTS: Artists interested in representation may send a letter with resumé and slides. Artists shown are selected based on saleability and proficiency/technique. Shows are scheduled three to four years in advance.

MIDDENDORF GALLERY

2009 Columbia Road, N.W.
Washington, DC 20009
(202)462-2009
Tuesday-Friday 11-6, Saturday 11-5
Member Washington Art Dealers Association

Owner: Christopher S. Middendorf
Director: Annie Gawlak
Price Range: $500 up
Cash, check, payment plan
Established 1974

In the Adams Morgan neighborhood, Middendorf Gallery shows a wide variety of art from the 19th century to the present, with an emphasis on major American artists.

Some of the most well-known artists in Washington are represented by Chris Middendorf, a handsome man who looks perhaps more like a 35-year-old law firm partner. Indeed, he studied at Harvard—but his degree is in art history. He thinks in some ways more like a graduate of the Business School. At any rate, he is one of the most passionate collectors around. He is always aware of what is saleable and what will probably prove to be the best investment.

Middendorf also provides corporate and private art consulting services.

MEDIA: Paintings, sculpture, photography; also drawings, original prints, collage, architectural, installations.

STYLES: Wide range of contemporary styles.

ARTISTS REGULARLY SHOWN: Washingtonians represented by Middendorf include: Sam Gilliam and the late Gene Davis (Washington Color School painters); William Christenberry (photographs and three-dimensional constructions often dealing with Southern and social commentary themes); Yuriko Yamaguchi. Also available are works by Ralston Crawford, William Eggleston, Richard Serra, Robert Longo, Manuel Neri (California figurative sculptor).

SELECTION OF NEW ARTISTS: Shows are scheduled from two months to two years in advance. Artists may send slides and a resumé. New artists are chosen based on originality, excellence of technique, and saleability and press record.

NEWMAN GALLERY

513 11th Street, S.E.
Washington, DC 20003
(202)544-7577
Tuesday-Saturday 10-6

Owner/Director: Michele Newman
Price Range: $30-2,000
Cash, check, MasterCard, Visa, payment plan
Established 1984

This tiny gallery, though known best for its quality framing services, frequently hosts one-person shows. Michele Newman is dedicated to the gallery facet of her business. Generally, relatively small works by new artists are featured.

Also, political cartoons are always available in the bin.

MEDIA: Paintings, drawings, prints.

STYLES: Traditional, including impressionist, expressionist, and a bit of naive.

ARTISTS REGULARLY SHOWN: Local artists. Newman apologized as she said that the gallery is too small to take on representation of artists.

SELECTION OF NEW ARTISTS: Artists are welcome to drop in with slides and/or actual work, phone for an appointment, or send a letter with slides. Shows are hung based on suitability of size (small), originality, and consistency.

NINTH STREET GALLERY

1553 9th Street, N.W.
Washington, DC 20001
(202)797-7488
Tuesday-Saturday 10-4

Owner/Director: S. Bruce Pascal
Price Range: $200-3,000
Cash, check
Established 1987

The beautifully renovated two-story townhouse now occupied by the newly opened Ninth Street Gallery once was a marble warehouse; not surprisingly, it is a large space with marble floors.

Bruce Pascal has an interesting story. A process server, he bought the building a year ago with the intention of using the back room as an office. A friend expressed interest in opening an art gallery in the front, and Pascal agreed. The friend abandoned ship, and Pascal is now the surprised owner of an art gallery. So far, he is both happy about it and very successful.

He says he will continue to showcase Washington area artists.

MEDIA: Paintings, drawings, sculpture, photography.

STYLES: Representational, expressionist, abstract-expressionist, experimental.

ARTISTS REGULARLY SHOWN: Linda Corridon, Tom Raneses, Marci Nadler, R. Neville Johnston (sculptures made from found objects including kitchen utensils), Marty Baird, Donald Davidson.

SELECTION OF NEW ARTISTS: Artists may phone for an appointment, or send a letter with slides and a resumé.

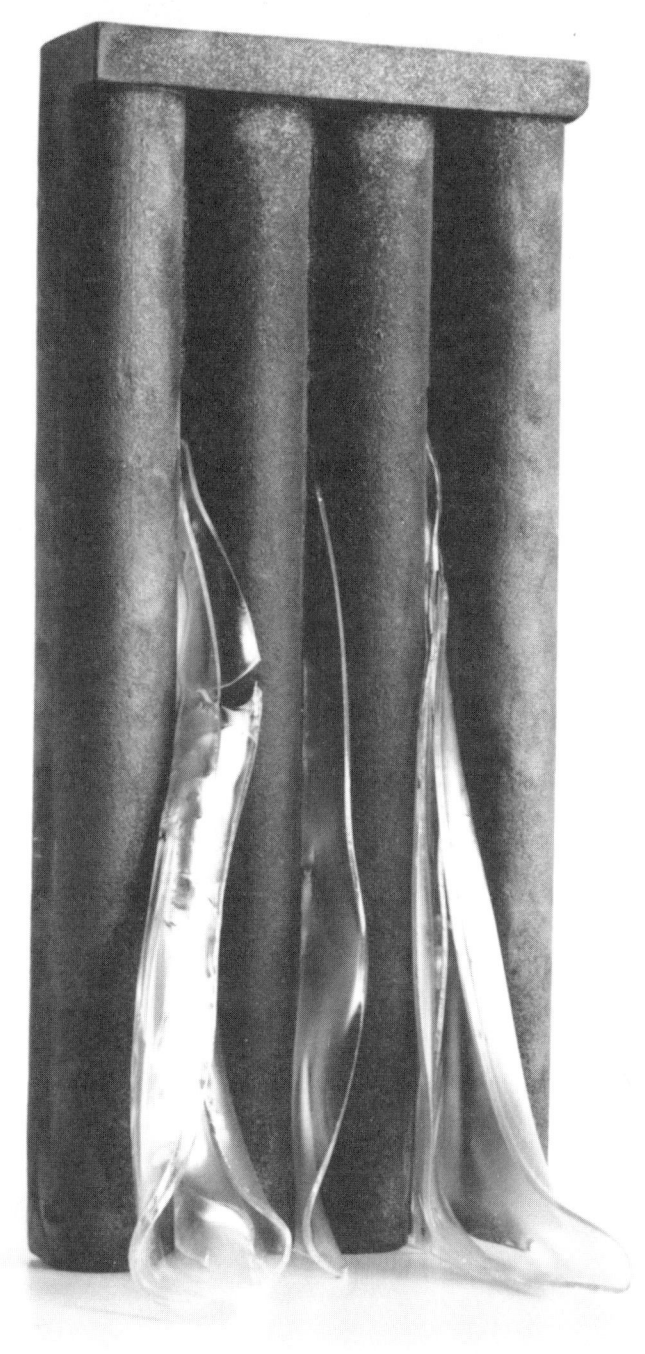

Paestum, 1986, by Mary Shaffer. Cast iron and slumped plate glass, 15"x7"x5". Anne O'Brien Gallery, page 56.

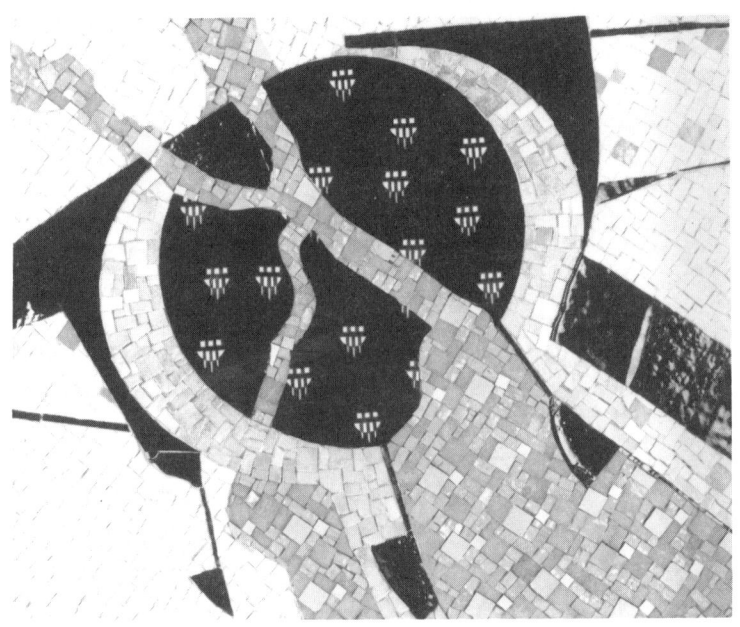

Kabuki, 1985, by Jerry W. Carter. Venetian glass, etched glass, gold leaf, marble, stone, 24"x30". Anne O'Brien Gallery.

ANNE O'BRIEN GALLERY

1701 Pennsylvania Avenue, N.W.
Washington, DC 20006
(202)429-9649
Tuesday-Saturday 10-6

Owner/Director: Marian A. O'Brien
Price Range: $100-6,000
Cash, check, American Express, payment plan
Established 1985

Anne O'Brien started out as a partner of a fine crafts shop in Georgetown before she decided to specialize in glass, which had always been of special interest to her.

Located in an airy mezzanine over the Franz Bader Gallery and a block from the Renwick, Anne O'Brien Gallery shows innovative, experimental work using glass and similar materials as the primary material. The glass art shown here might be a sculptural construction, a mosaic, or even a painting incorporating glass.

MEDIA: Glass works in both two- and three-dimensional forms.

STYLES: Abstract, expressionist, experimental, conceptual; also, some architectural glass. Commissions can be arranged.

ARTISTS REGULARLY SHOWN: Contemporary glass artists from around the world are represented, including Stephen Paul Day (bronze castings with glass); Jon F. Clark (large-scale mold-blown glass); Bonnie Biggs (figurative ink wash drawings within laminated glass); Janusz A. Walengynowicz (paintings with cast glass and oils on wood); John Gilbert Luebtow (architectural glass—sandblasted and slumped plate glass); Lynn Hally Olivetti (landscapes; natural glass and plexiglass). Washington artists include Jerry Carter (mosaics), Jeffrey Chapline (cast glass), Mary Shaffer (slumped glass with metal or stone).

SELECTION OF NEW ARTISTS: Artists may send slides with a cover letter, and they may submit with the intention of being in a group show rather than a solo show. Shows are scheduled at least one year in advance. The gallery sponsors new talent shows.

OLD WARSAW GALLERIES

319 Cameron Street
Alexandria, VA 22314
(703)548-9188
Tuesday-Saturday 11-6, Sunday 12-6

Owner/Director: Barbara Witulska-Lazo
Cash, check, MasterCard, Visa,
American Express
Established 1974

In spite of the word "Old" being in the name of this gallery, Old Warsaw handles mostly new work. This gallery specializes in the work of contemporary Polish artists from the Old Country and around the world. Barbara Witulska-Lazo feels that Polish artists have long been short-changed by the circumstances and politics of wars, and oppressed in general. Her ongoing intention is to bring outstanding Polish art to the U.S.

Old Warsaw takes up the first floor of an Old Town Alexandria townhouse. Available work includes contemporary and semi-antique paintings and prints. Unique to Washington is jewelry made with sterling silver settings and "gold of the north," or amber from the Baltic Sea. These stones often contain moss or chalk, creating very interesting effects.

The gallery regularly sponsors slide lectures by artists and receptions honoring Polish writers and other notables. A gift shop offers some hand-made folk crafts and other items. A small selection of books, cards, and multiples are available as well.

MEDIA: Paintings; drawings; sculpture; original prints; artist books; crafts in media including ceramic, wood, fiber art, and jewelry.

STYLES: Representational, impressionist, naive, surrealist, abstract, expressionist. Commissions can be arranged.

ARTISTS REGULARLY SHOWN: Represented artists include: Polish artists born in and living in Poland; artists born in Poland but living abroad; and artists of Polish extraction born and/or living elsewhere.

SELECTION OF NEW ARTISTS: Artists of the appropriate ethnic background may send a letter with slides and recommendations.

OSUNA GALLERY

406 7th Street, N.W.
Washington, DC 20004
(202)296-1963
Tuesday-Saturday 10-5
Member Washington Art Dealers Association

Owner/Director: Ramon Osuna
Manager: Helen Harper
Established 1963

Located in The 406, Osuna Gallery—once known as Pyramid—is on the second floor down the hall from Jane Haslem. Generally, contemporary work is shown here.

However, Ramon Osuna's taste in art runs the gamut from realistic to highly abstract works. "I show what I like," he says; "That's why my gallery is eclectic. I like contemporary work, I like Old Masters." In fact, on a regular basis Osuna hangs a show of stunning paintings by the Old and 19th century masters and their followers. Viewings of such works can be arranged year-round. Osuna has also been known to have available artwork from South and Latin America by such notables as Diego Rivera. These masterwork shows are accompanied by illustrated catalogs.

MEDIA: Paintings, drawings, sculpture.

STYLES: Abstract, minimalist, Washington Color School, representational.

ARTISTS REGULARLY SHOWN: Rebecca Davenport (contemporary social realist painter), W. C. Richardson, Manon Cleary (photorealist paintings), John Van Alstine, Anne Truitt (minimalist painted sculpture), Ann Purcell, Peter Dean, Aaron Levine, Carol Goldberg (brightly painted cut-out figures and plant forms; folding screens).

SELECTION OF NEW ARTISTS: Osuna is not interested in reviewing portfolios at this time.

PARTNERS GALLERY

4724 Hampden Lane
Bethesda, MD 20814
(301)657-2781
Tuesday-Saturday 10-6 (Friday 10-8)

Owner/Directors: Dana Cohen and
Susan Turner
Cash, check, MasterCard, Visa,
American Express, payment plan
Established 1987

Susan Turner, one of the partners of Partners, directed the antique/art gallery The Best of Everything before teaming with Dana Cohen to form Partners. This new gallery has indeed formed a partnership with some of the best contemporary realist painters in the country.

But the multi-level, handsomely designed interior architecture of the gallery enables Partners to exhibit several kinds of art at the same time in a way that works. Three-dimensional work including ceramic and jewelry pieces punctuate and complement adjacent paintings.

Partners Gallery is just off the inner courtyard in One Bethesda Center. Carved brick architectural sculpture/ornamentation by Mara Smith is near the door; Smith's work is also incorporated elsewhere in the complex.

MEDIA: Paintings, sculpture, crafts, wearables.

STYLES: Paintings: primarily contemporary realism, from photorealism to classical techniques to somewhat loosely-painted, surrealist, or naive styles; also, some abstract styles.

ARTISTS REGULARLY SHOWN: Represented artists include: Susan Contreras; Robert Striffolino; Clarinda Jennison; Terry P. Rodgers (photorealist painter featured on the December 1986 cover of *American Artist);* Frank Holmes; James Tormey; Sue Wall; Jamie Baxter; James Eaton.

SELECTION OF NEW ARTISTS: Artists may send a letter with slides and resumé. Shows are scheduled more than one year in advance.

PICTURESQUE

10132 Colvin Run Road
Great Falls, VA 22066
(703)759-0152
Tuesday-Saturday 10-6

Owners: Tracy Sparks, Nghia Pham
Price Range: $50-600
Cash, check, MasterCard, Visa,
payment plan
Established 1986

This tiny gallery is in a new business townhouse center at the corner of Walker Road and Colvin Run Road. Tracy Sparks and Nghia Pham derive most of their income from the museum-quality, custom framing facility, but they take the gallery aspect of their business seriously. The treasures available here could justify a drive to the country.

Among other media, some miniature monoprints at giveaway prices are available. Other original hand-pulled prints as well as signed offsets are available in the rack.

MEDIA: Paintings, pastels, drawings, prints, photographs, original book illustrations, cast and painted paper, signed offsets.

STYLES: Representational to lyrically abstract.

ARTISTS REGULARLY SHOWN: Pat Berlin, Jamie Brooks, Pauline Lorfano, Michael Stewart, Lassie Corbett, Marian Buckner, Jane Louise McGavin, Judith Hill Shea, Ellen Walle Haberlein, Suzanne Twyford.

SELECTION OF NEW ARTISTS: Interested artists may phone for an appointment. New artists are selected based primarily on originality, saleability, and technique.

PLUM GALLERY

3762 Howard Avenue
Kensington, MD 20895
(301)933-0222
Tuesday-Saturday 11-4

Partners: Paula Locker, Lillian Mones,
and Muriel Miller
Price Range: $100-10,000
Cash, check, payment plan
Established 1976

Although the Plum Gallery is on the second floor of a building in the Kensington antiques complex, it has handled contemporary work for years. Both locally and nationally recognized artists are represented.

The work shown here is generally colorful and rather large. It is always well-crafted, highly original work which merits attention.

MEDIA: Contemporary paintings, prints, sculpture, artists' paper and collage, jewelry, ceramics.

STYLES: Abstract, abstract expressionist.

ARTISTS REGULARLY SHOWN: Val Lewton, Lawrence Heyman, William Calfee (sculpture), Helen Frederick (printmaker, also director of Pyramid Atlantic), Patricia Friend (paintings), Helen Corning.

SELECTION OF NEW ARTISTS: Interested artists may phone for an appointment, or send a letter with slides, resumé, and recommendations. New artists are selected based primarily on originality, technique, and consistency. Shows are scheduled up to two years in advance.

THE REGENCY GALLERY INC.

(202)547-8646
Monday-Friday 10-6; Saturday 10:30-4
   and by appointment
New location opening soon—call for details

Owner/Director: Lewis Fields
Price Range: $300 up
Cash, check, payment plan
Established 1986

Lewis Fields has succeeded in many areas of endeavor. A collector, he bought his first painting for $6,000 in 1952; he could afford it because he was playing professional ice hockey. Later, on the heels of a career in journalism and public relations, he founded *Performance*, a playbill with a national readership.

Fields's overflowing collection led to his opening a gallery. He is fascinated by classical Surrealism; he also has expertise in contemporary black artists.

The Regency Gallery offers graphic design, curatorial, and acquisitions services.

MEDIA: Paintings, works on paper, sculpture, photography, original prints.

STYLES: Traditional, representational, impressionist, abstract expressionist, Western, surrealist, and contemporary black art. Commissions can be arranged.

ARTISTS REGULARLY SHOWN: About 20-40 artists are regularly shown, including: Fran Stetina (hand-colored photographs), Richard Dempsey, Lois Mailou Jones, Delilah Pierce, James L. Wells, James DuPree, David Zimmerman (light-filled, brilliantly colored representational paintings), Thomas Hart Benton. Look for works by Jacob Lawrence, Romare Bearden, and other major artists in future shows.

SELECTION OF NEW ARTISTS: Artists interested in representation may phone for an appointment. Criteria for the selection of new artists include professionalism of technique, originality of vision, and consistency in work.

HOLLY ROSS ASSOCIATES GALLERY

516 C Street, N.E.
Washington, DC 20002
(202)544-0400
Tuesday-Friday 11-5, Saturday 10-3,
   and by appointment

Owner: Holly Ross
Director: Sheryl Ameen
Cash, check, payment plan
Established 1981

Holly Ross Associates Gallery, on Capitol Hill, is in the oldest frame townhouse in Washington. The front belies the large amount of space inside.

A variety of work is available. Holly Ross and her staff also offer art consulting and custom framing services. They are willing to go to the client's home or business establishment to advise on art acquisition, placement, and framing.

MEDIA: Paintings, drawings, sculpture, photography, original prints, collage, crafts, handmade paper.

STYLES: Traditional, representational, impressionist, abstract expressionist, minimalist, surrealist, conceptual, pop. Commissions can be arranged.

ARTISTS REGULARLY SHOWN: Alexis de Boeck (Washington painter), Jim Sundquist (Washington printmaker), Bill Dunlap (Virginia painter), LeJune (French realist printmaker), Ali Faili (Washington painter), Sirpa Yarmolinsky (paper and mixed media), Tom Holland, Chuck Close.

SELECTION OF NEW ARTISTS: Artists interested in representation may phone for an appointment, or may send slides with resumé and recommendations. Criteria for the selection of new artists include proficiency of technique and saleability.

JACK SHAINMAN GALLERY

2443 18th Street, N.W.
Washington, DC 20009
(202)462-3497
Wednesday-Saturday 11-7,
Sunday 2-6, and by appointment

Owner: Jack Shainman
Director: Kimberly Martin
Price Range: $600 up
Cash, check, payment plan
Established 1984

Jack Shainman Gallery is a large, high-ceilinged space in Adams Morgan.
Jack Shainman also operates a gallery in SoHo. "I know and enjoy exploring the best of recent cutting edge art which combines original content and formal excellence," Shainman says. Being in two important cities, he feels that he can "actively monitor new directions in contemporary art." He expresses dedication to the progress of the visual arts, but commitment to keeping track of relevant work, not trends. Often he runs concurrent shows in both galleries.
  MEDIA: Paintings, sculpture, photography.
  STYLES: No set style; high quality, cutting edge.
  ARTISTS REGULARLY SHOWN: 16 American and international artists, including: Evergon (large format Polaroids), Paul Bowen (sculpture). Painters: Deborah Remington, Arnold Mesches, Aaron Fink, Stewart Hitch, Dale Frank, Robert McCurdy, Claude Simard, Steven Cushner, Bruno Ceccobelli.
  SELECTION OF NEW ARTISTS: Shainman is not currently interested in reviewing portfolios.

SPECTRUM GALLERY

Please refer to the next chapter, Cooperative Galleries.

STUDIO GALLERY

Please refer to the next chapter, Cooperative Galleries.

Lamp from Midway Gardens, Chicago, c. 1913, designed by Frank Lloyd Wright. Tartt Gallery.

THE TARTT GALLERY

2017 Q Street, N.W.
Washington, DC 20009
(202)332-5652
Tuesday-Saturday 11-5
Member Dupont Circle Fine Art Galleries

Owner/Director: Jo C. Tartt, Jr.
Price Range: $100 up
Cash, check
Established 1986

During his 10 years as rector of Grace Episcopal Church in Georgetown, Jo Tartt avidly collected and practiced photography. In 1981 Tartt left the rectory to become a private dealer, and by 1985 he decided to open a gallery in two stories of the large Victorian townhouse he was renovating. His inaugural exhibit opened on Valentine's Day 1986 accompanied by a record snow, crowds nonetheless, and supportive press coverage which this gallery has continued to earn by showing interesting, sometimes disturbing, but always high quality art.

The front room features a colorful ceiling construction by Washington architect/sculptor Dickson Carroll—this unusual architectural treatment is worth a visit in itself. Its excellent craftsmanship yet whimsy reflect the natures of both Jo Tartt and his gallery.

MEDIA: Emphasis on 19th and 20th century American and European photography. Also, contemporary paintings, sculpture, and artists' books by national and Washington area artists; decorative arts (see plate above—this Frank Lloyd Wright design is the only known surviving lamp from Midway Gardens in Chicago), and finally a collection of contemporary folk art.

STYLES: Photographic techniques, traditional and innovative styles; decorative; figurative/abstract-expressionist; folk; more. Eclectic.

ARTISTS REGULARLY SHOWN: Terry Braunstein (color photomontages), Lee Haner (paintings with almost International Icon-like heiroglyphs), Robyn Johnson-Ross (paintings), Arnold Kramer (photographs), Reginald Pollack (paintings and sculpture), and Genna Watson (sculpture).

SELECTION OF NEW ARTISTS: Artists may send slides, recommendations, and a resumé. New artists are selected based primarily on originality/content, consistency in work, and professional presentation. Shows are scheduled up to a year in advance.

TOUCHSTONE GALLERY

Please refer to the next chapter, Cooperative Galleries.

VEERHOFF GALLERIES

1604 17th Street, N.W.
Washington, DC 20009
(202)387-2322
Tuesday-Saturday 9:30-6

Owner/Director: Margaret Veerhoff
Price Range: $100-5,000
Cash, check, MasterCard, Visa,
American Express, payment plan
Established 1871

Veerhoff Galleries is the oldest commercial gallery in Washington. Margaret Veerhoff is the great granddaughter of William Veerhoff, the cabinetmaker/framer who founded the gallery in 1871. Museum quality custom framing is still offered here along with restoration services.

Veerhoff says, "Generally speaking, when we show contemporary art it is by realist local artists. We also have a large selection of old prints and paintings." The old graphics may at any time include Thomas Nast cartoons; Audubon prints; and work by little-known artists including maps and prints of Washington scenes. European works are available too.

She especially enjoys selling art to people who fall in love with a particular piece, and she makes it easy for a client to get to know art. Knowing that sometimes "It is hard to decide," she offers a two-week approval policy for clients who would like to take a piece home and try it. She will also take work back later in trade.

MEDIA: Paintings; drawings; sculpture in terra cotta, stone, and bronze; graphics, antique to contemporary.

STYLES: Realist. Commissions can be arranged.

ARTISTS REGULARLY SHOWN: Several contemporary artists are regularly shown, including: Helen Hoffman (pastels and paintings); Rick Biehl (silkscreen); Audrey Preissler Roll (sculpture); Bill Tilton (alkyd paintings); and watercolorists Barbara Preston, Teryl Speers, and Carmen Sherbeck.

SELECTION OF NEW ARTISTS: Artists interested in representation may phone for an appointment. Criteria for the selection of new artists include saleability, proficiency of realistic technique, and consistency in work. The four annual one-person shows are booked a year in advance.

The Color Plates

Rocks at Narragansett, c. 1863, by William Stanley Haseltine. Oil on canvas, 12"x22". Adams Davidson Gallery, page 102.

Lady with Georgian Clasp on Pearl Choker, 1985, by Judy Horowitz. Oil on panel, 10"x8". Photograph by Joel Breger. Portrait Connection, page 166.

Spin Whirl II, 1986, by Agnes Jacobs. Painted construction, 39"x42"x7". Photograph by Ed Owens. B. R. Kornblatt Gallery, page 48.

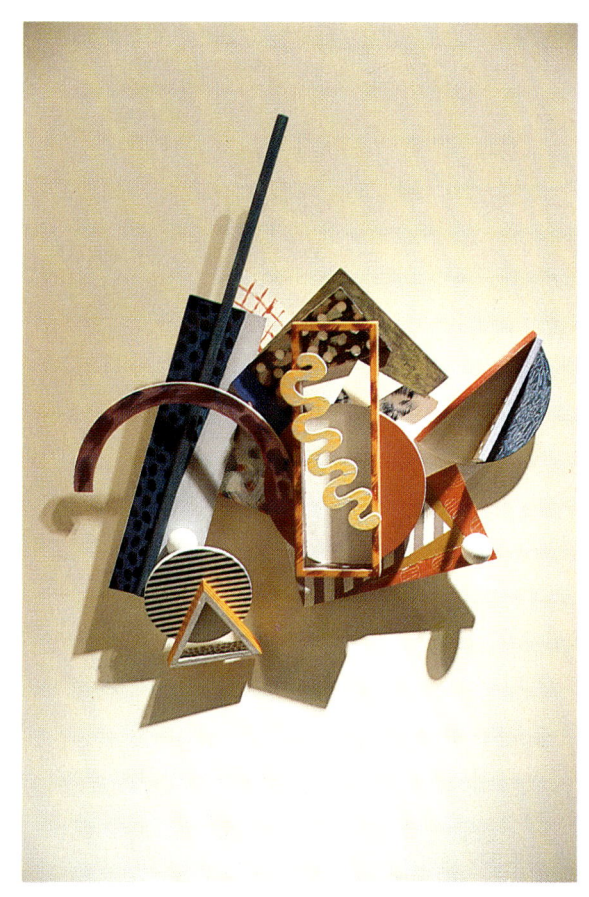

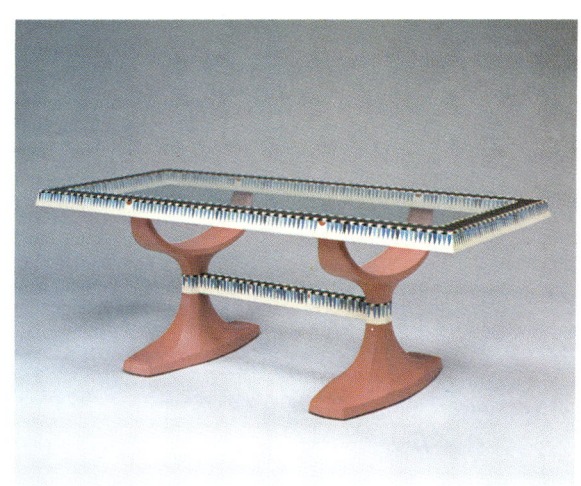

Pharaoh's Table, 1987, by Peter Dean. Holly and ebony, watercolored and lacquered. Mogul Gallery, page 88.

On the C&O Canal, 1986, by Wolf Kahn. Oil on canvas, 44"x60". Photograph by Sarah Wells. B. R. Kornblatt Gallery, page 48.

Beneath the Birch Trees, 1987, by Margaret Alderson. Mixed, 28"x36". Studio 7, Torpedo Factory Art Center, page 151.

Three Tents, 1986, by Frederick McDuff. Oil on linen, 11"x16".
Venable Neslage Galleries, page 65.

Christ, 1986, by Angelos. Oil on canvas, 71"x31 1/2". Photograph by Manolis Vernardos. Zygos Gallery, page 72.

Cat, 1985, by Manolis Polymeris. Oil on panel, 39 1/2"x27 1/2". Photograph by Manolis Vernardos. Zygos Gallery, page 72.

Morning Mist, 1986, by Tseng-Ying Pang. Serigraph, 26"x18 1/2". Gallerie Julian, page 96.

VENABLE NESLAGE GALLERIES
[See Color Plate after page 64]

1803 Connecticut Avenue, N.W.
Washington, DC 20009
(202)462-1800
Tuesday-Saturday 10-6

Owner: Oliver J. Neslage
Director: John R. Stromberg
Price Range: $400-10,000
Cash, check, MasterCard, Visa,
American Express, payment plan
Established 1892

Established in 1892 by Samuel J. Venable, Venable Neslage is the second oldest gallery in Washington. Oliver J. Neslage took over as the gallery's president in 1963 and steered it into its current direction: the paintings and graphics of contemporary impressionist artists. Frederick H. McDuff III, an impressionist painter, is a vice president of the gallery as well as Artist in Residence.

The gallery has two storeys; the second floor features changing exhibits. Museum quality custom framing is offered.

MEDIA: Paintings, drawings, sculpture, original prints.

STYLES: Contemporary but generally traditional, including representational and impressionist.

ARTISTS REGULARLY SHOWN: Frederick McDuff, Joseph Sheppard (one of the finest living realist painters), Lillian August, Yury Kokoyanin (paintings, etchings), Marcelle Stoianovich, William Schmidt, Nina Akamu, Meg Egeberg, Mario Micossi.

SELECTION OF NEW ARTISTS: Artists may send a letter with resumé and slides. Artists are chosen based primarily on proficiency of technique, saleability, and consistency. Shows are scheduled up to a year in advance.

THE VILLAGE GALLERY OF GREAT FALLS

718 Walker Road
Great Falls, VA 22066
(703)759-3209
Monday-Saturday 11-5, Sunday 1-5

Owner/Director: Nelson F. Getchell
Price Range: $350-5,000
Cash, check, MasterCard, Visa, payment plan
Established 1970

The Village Gallery is an antique shop. But on the walls complementing the collectibles are delightful original watercolors by the British book illustrator Roy Gerrard, and smaller paintings by Elizabeth Finn, who is also English.

STYLES: Representational: fantasy, landscape, illustrative, nature, nautical.

SELECTION OF NEW ARTISTS: Artists are welcome to call for an appointment. Nelson Getchell works with a very few "serious developing artists" whom he chooses based on proficiency of technique, professionalism, and originality.

WALKER, URSITTI & McGINNISS GALLERY

457 M Street, N.W.
Washington, DC 20001
(202)737-7445
Wednesday-Saturday 12-6,
and by appointment

Owners: J. Shepherd Walker; Christopher F.
Ursitti; Paul E. McGinniss, Director
Price Range: Up to $8,000
Cash, check, payment plan
Established 1985

Walker, Ursitti & McGinniss are not lawyers, they are artists; but it is possible that they are poking fun at Washington because their gallery name sounds more like that of a law firm.

Actually, they deliberately sited their gallery several blocks away from other galleries, in an emerging part of town, partly to share art with people who might not normally venture into commercial galleries. The directors espouse a "populist philosophy with an egalitarian aesthetic"—this boils down to a belief in the basic equality of all people, and that art is for everybody.

The gallery is in a three-story Victorian rowhouse and consists of 2,500 sq. ft. of exhibit space. In front of the gallery, a carved wood preacher clad in black suit and skinny white tie looms out of the yard. He is holding the Bible and his arm is outstretched in a gesture of blessing.

MEDIA: Work shown here is often experimental. Showing "all forms and fashions of quality contemporary art," the gallery mounts shows of traditional two- and three-dimensional media but also ventures into video, installations, and performance art. It is perhaps the only commercial gallery in the city which has ventured into the latter three media, although some alternative art centers have too.

STYLES: A wide variety of contemporary art; anything well-crafted and striking.

ARTISTS REGULARLY SHOWN: 30 artists are shown in a given year, including Chuang, Costas, Flickinger, Gabbay, Gardner, Majercak, Mullany, New, Newcombe, Robért.

SELECTION OF NEW ARTISTS: Artists interested in representation may send a letter with slides. New artists are chosen based on originality of content, proficiency of technique, and professional presentation. Given the size of the gallery, volume of work can also be a factor, although artists may submit with the intention of being in a group show. Shows are scheduled six months to one year ahead of time.

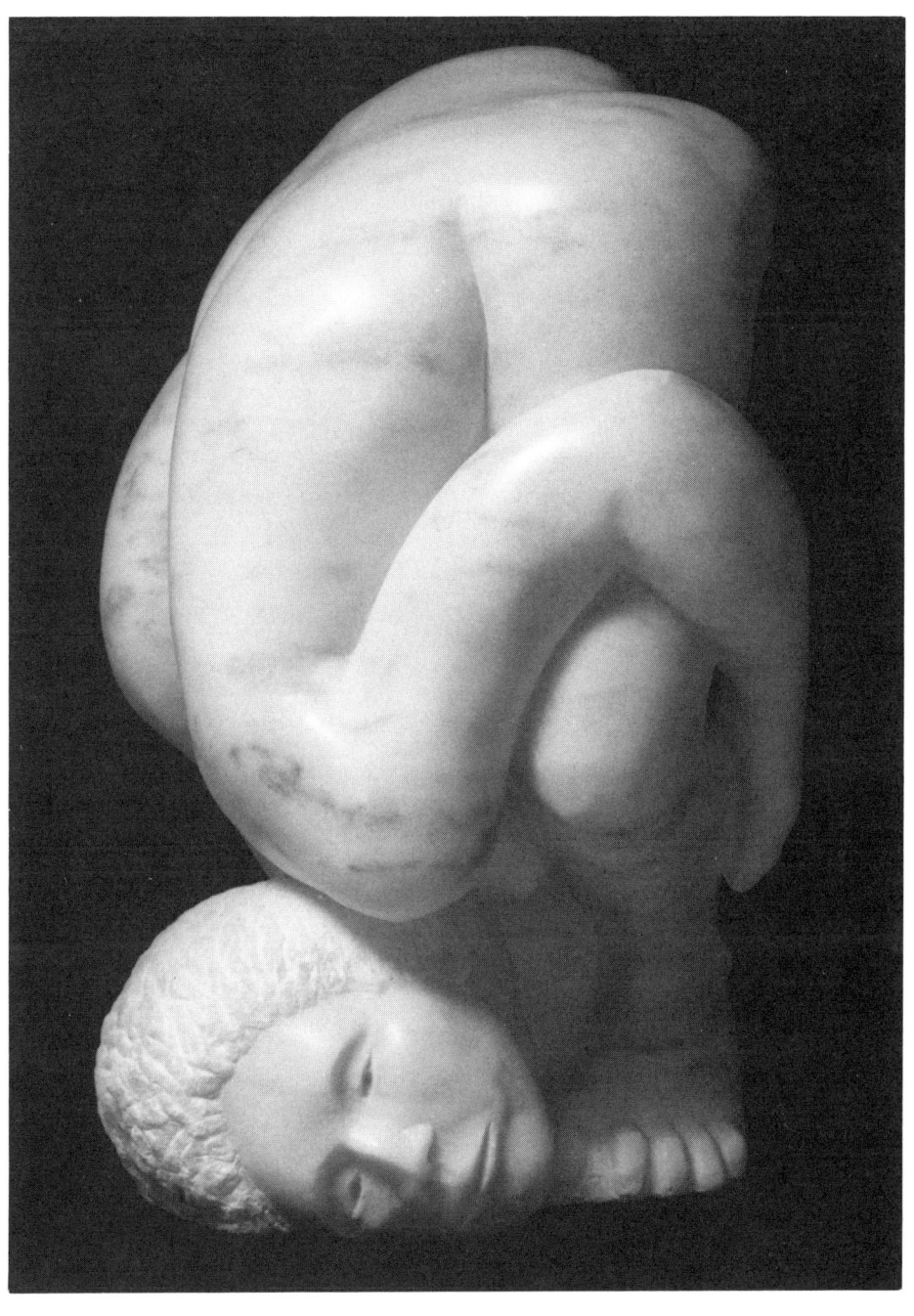

White Buffalo Woman and the Last Flower, 1983, by M. C. Carolyn.
Marble, 23"x14"x13". Photograph by Joel Breger.
Wallace Wentworth Gallery, page 68.

WALLACE WENTWORTH GALLERY

2006 R Street, N.W.
Washington, DC 20009
(202)387-7152
Tuesday-Saturday 11-6
and by appointment
Member Dupont Circle Fine Art Galleries

Owners: Ansley Wallace
and Eric Wentworth
Cash, check, MasterCard, Visa, payment plan
Established 1984

Located in a three-story townhouse in Dupont Circle, this spacious gallery shows an astonishing variety of contemporary work.

Some of the shows are relatively risky. For example, a recent solo show called "Stations" featured abstract paintings by Anne Marchand, inspired by the Stations of the Cross. In fact, a healthy proporation of Wallace Wentworth Gallery's artwork is spiritual and mystical in orientation.

But all the work available here is eclectic and highly interesting. Some of it is high tech, incorporating electronic and light elements. Ansley Wallace and Eric Wentworth have even begun to explore the field of recent masters; occasional works by Cassatt, Pollock, and others appear.

The first floor features changing shows; a large inventory of work is available on the other two floors. One represented artist said, "They are willing to try new and unusual works and themes. That is why I appreciate showing there."

MEDIA: Paintings, works on paper, sculpture, architectural, collage.

STYLES: Representational, impressionist, abstract, expressionist, experimental.

ARTISTS REGULARLY SHOWN: Artists from around the country and Europe are represented, including Dorothy Hood (lyrical abstraction), John Dickson (sculpture incorporating found objects), M.C. Carolyn (marble and stone sculpture), Alice Lees, (neon), Danville Chadbourne (ritualistic work), Judy Chicago, Clyde Lynds (stelae with changing fiber optics).

SELECTION OF NEW ARTISTS: Wallace and Wentworth prefer to discover new artists themselves through referrals and studio visits.

WASHINGTON GALLERY OF FINE ARTS

1531 33rd Street, N.W.
Washington, DC 20007
(202)333-8199
Monday-Saturday 10-5

Owner/Director: Robert La Vita
Assistant Director: Claude de Morelos
Price Range: $400-5,000
Cash, check, payment plan
Established 1987

The Washington Gallery of Fine Arts takes up the first floor of a high-ceilinged townhouse a block west of Wisconsin Avenue at 33rd and Volta Place.

When Robert La Vita, an interior architect, first opened this gallery early in 1987, he specialized in 19th century paintings and sculpture. However, he is now handling traditionally executed representational work by contemporary artists.

MEDIA: Paintings, works on paper, sculpture.

STYLES: New realist, neo-impressionist, new luminist. Color and light are important to La Vita.

ARTISTS REGULARLY SHOWN: Artists from around the country and Europe are represented: Felix Nunez Molinero (new impressionist from Spain); Claude Menard de Morelos (Washington artist though French-born); Steven Meyers (Washington area sculptor who studied in Europe).

SELECTION OF NEW ARTISTS: Artists are welcome to telephone for an appointment, drop in with slides and/or actual work, or send a letter with slides. Work is selected based on consistency, technique, and originality.

WASHINGTON PRINTMAKERS GALLERY

Please refer to the next chapter, Cooperative Galleries.

WATERGATE GALLERY

Watergate Mall
2552 Virginia Avenue, N.W.
Washington, DC 20037
(202)338-4451
Monday-Saturday 10-6

Owner/Director: Dale Johnson
Cash, check, MasterCard, Visa,
American Express, payment plan
Established 1980

Although known primarily as a custom framing facility, Watergate Gallery and Frame Design also features local artists working in all media as long as the work is fairly small.

MEDIA: Paintings, works on paper, sculpture, prints.

STYLES: Fairly conservative styles, from representational to abstract.

ARTISTS REGULARLY SHOWN: Local artists.

SELECTION OF NEW ARTISTS: Artists are welcome to telephone for an appointment, or send a letter with slides. Work is selected based on consistency, technique, and originality.

WINSTON GALLERY

1204 31st Street, N.W.
Washington, DC 20007
(202)333-5414
Tuesday-Saturday 10-6

Owner/Director: Nancy Stevenson
Price Range: $1,000-50,000
Cash, check
Established 1986

Winston Gallery was established "to promote fine contemporary painting and sculpture." Nancy Stevenson, formerly Lieutenant Governor of South Carolina, collects contemporary art. She found that the artwork in her personal collection generated interest and openness in others. In her relatively new capacity as a gallery director, she takes great joy in continuing to bring art and people together.

A large gallery near the corner of 31st and M, Winston is able to showcase large work effectively. The gallery also has a small room featuring more intimate works. Some of Stevenson's artists are in major museum collections, and some are emerging artists.

MEDIA: Paintings, drawings, sculpture.

STYLES: Primarily abstract including expressionist, minimalist, abstract-expressionist; some representational work as well.

ARTISTS REGULARLY SHOWN: The work of 25 artists is available, including: Peter Brown (painted wood wall sculpture); Robert Gil de Montes (expressionist oil paintings); Caroline Orner (foil and wax emulsion, spiritual subjects); Jenny Snider (psychological oil paintings); Paul Daniel (aluminum and steel painted kinetic sculpure); Colin Thomson (abstract oil paintings); Richard Lew (stone sculpture and construction); Marilyn Mahoney (abstract drawings and paintings); Bill Barratte (acrylic resin and metal wall pieces).

SELECTION OF NEW ARTISTS: Artists interested in representation may send a letter with slides, resumé, and recommendations. New artists are chosen primarily based on proficiency of technique, originality, and consistency.

ZENITH GALLERY

Gallery Row
413 7th Street, N.W.
Washington, DC 20004
(202)783-2963
Wednesday-Saturday 11-6
Member Washington Art Dealers Association

Owner/Director: Margery Goldberg
Price Range: $15-6,000
Cash, check, MasterCard, Visa,
payment plan
Established 1978

Zenith Gallery, formerly located on Rhode Island Avenue, N.W., opened a second space at Gallery Row in 1987. Partly because of controversial zoning disputes at the first location, and also because the new location has been so well-received, Margery Goldberg decided to close the original location and concentrate on the new one.

The applicable words for Zenith are "eclectic" and often "smile." A wide variety of highly original, sometimes quirky artwork is available, from jewelry to large-scale paintings. Also, Zenith, one of the few galleries to feature neon art, sponsors an annual group show of neon artists.

MEDIA: All painting media, sculpture, fine crafts, works on paper, original prints, collage, neon.

STYLES: Range from representational to impressionist to experimental, abstract, and conceptual. The work shown here is hard to pin down; it is usually energetic, often whimsical, and always well-crafted.

ARTISTS REGULARLY SHOWN: 20-30 artists are shown regularly, including: Chas Colburn (steel sculpture), Ann Hanson (whimsical celluclay animal sculptures), Fran Larsen (watercolors with hand-carved and -painted frames), Carol Newmyer (jewelry and small bronzes with movable pieces), Guenther Riess (three-dimensional paper constructions), Hal Larsen, and Todd Warner (whimsical animal sculptures).

SELECTION OF NEW ARTISTS: Artists may send slides with a resumé and recommendations or call for an appointment. Artists are chosen based on originality, consistency, proficiency, and technical ability. The gallery also sponsors new talent shows.

Two Female Figures, c. 1940, by G. Gounaro. Charcoal on paper, 12³/4"x17³/4". Zygos Gallery.

ZYGOS GALLERY
[See Color Plates after page 64]

403 7th Street, N.W.
Washington, DC 20004
(202)347-7740
Tuesday-Saturday 10:30-5:30
Sunday 12-5
Affiliated with Zygos Gallery in
Athens, Greece, est. 1956

Owner: Hellenic Arts, Inc.
Director: Ion F. Frantzeskakis
Price Range: $500-25,000
Cash, check, American Express, payment plan
Established 1986

Ion Frantzeskakis grew up surrounded by Greek art and artists. The son of an art dealer, he developed a passionate desire to share Greek contemporary culture with other parts of the world. After exploring other cities in Europe and the United States, Frantzeskakis settled in Washington, D.C. because he feels that "the city was built on a human scale and shows great potential for growth into a major visual arts center."

Zygos Gallery exhibits artwork by maturing contemporary Greek artists. Opposed to the "merchant mentality" of "pushing" works by stars whose high-priced markets have already been established, Frantzeskakis wishes to expose fine art to those people who are willing to buy fairly priced new work for its intrinsic quality and beauty.

Although Frantzeskakis's expertise is in contemporary Greek art, some of the nine solo shows hung each year feature American artists.

MEDIA: Paintings, works on paper, sculpture, original prints, photographs, collage, mosaic, jewelry.

STYLES: Work shown covers much ground stylistically: surrealist, spiritual, abstract-expressionist, realist, impressionist.

ARTISTS REGULARLY SHOWN: About 30 artists are shown per year, including: Polymeris (abstract expressionist oil paintings), Kamavas, Angelos (realist oil paintings), Mortarakos, Gounaro, Dionatos, Lambrinos (medium- to large-scale paintings of beautiful and vivid color), Papayannis, Kouris, Mavrommati.

SELECTION OF NEW ARTISTS: Artists interested in representation are encouraged to phone for an appointment, but are also welcome to drop in with slides, resumé, and perhaps a couple of examples of actual work.

Cooperatives

A SALON

R Street Gallery
The Jackson School Arts Center
R Street, N.W. between 30th and 31st
Washington, DC 20007
(202)337-4888
Thursday 4-9, Friday-Sunday 12-5

Artists' Cooperative
Director: Josephine Simonds
Sales referred to artist
Established 1979

    A Salon is a cross between an artists' cooperative and a membership art center. Like a co-op, it is entirely artist-run—members make all decisions, plan and execute all exhibits and programs, gallery-sit, administer the gallery, etc. But unlike most cooperatives, anyone can join; there is no jury process. Two different levels of membership are offered. Full members ($25/month) are entitled to a one-person show every year or two, and they may rent a studio through the A Salon program. Associate members ($45/year) may participate in several group shows. Occasionally juried shows are sponsored to make A Salon's galleries available to non-member artists.
    The Takoma Metro Arts Center is largely the result of the efforts of George Koch, one of the co-founders and a present officer of A Salon. Some A Salon members maintain studios there, and the Salon oversees a gallery there which is rented out.
    MEDIA: Two- and three-dimensional media including painting, drawing, sculpture, original prints, collage, constructions.
    STYLES: All contemporary styles from representational to highly abstract.
    ARTISTS REGULARY SHOWN: There are over 150 members. Contact the gallery for the full list of artists.
    SELECTION OF NEW ARTISTS: Call either location to find out when the next meeting is. Membership is open. $25/month or $45/year, depending on membership.

CITY GALLERY

1083 Wisconsin Avenue, N.W.
Washington, DC 20007
(202)338-2489
Wednesday-Saturday 11-6, Sunday 12-5

Artists' Cooperative
Director: Deborah A. Dubinski
Cash, check, MasterCard, Visa, payment plan
Established 1987

    Founded by an architect/sculptor and other artists, this brand-new second-story gallery is at the corner of Wisconsin Avenue and M Street, N.W. in Georgetown. It is a gallery which could fall into several categories—basically it is a cooperative, as 40 artists are member/owners.
    However, they have hired a part-time director, and they are actively soliciting proposals from other artists. City's intention is to promote Washington area artists.
    The front room features one-person shows; the other four rooms feature changing group shows.
    MEDIA: Most two- and three-dimensional media.
    STYLES: All contemporary styles from traditional to highly abstract.
    ARTISTS REGULARLY SHOWN: City has over 40 members. Contact the gallery for the full artist list.
    SELECTION OF NEW ARTISTS: Artists are invited to send a letter with slides, resumé, and recommendations. The initial membership fee is $125, then dues are $65 per month. Members must gallery-sit four hours per month. Shows are scheduled about six months in advance.

ENAMELISTS

This cooperative gallery specializes in enamel work. See the Torpedo Factory Art Center, in the Art Centers chapter.

FACTORY PHOTOWORKS

This cooperative gallery, specializing in photography, is located within the Torpedo Factory Art Center. See the latter's listing in the Art Centers chapter.

FIBER GALLERY

This cooperative gallery specializes in wearables. See the Torpedo Factory Art Center in the Art Centers chapter.

FOUNDRY GALLERY

9 Hillyer Court, N.W.
Washington, DC 20008
(202)387-0203
Tuesday-Saturday 11-5, Sunday 1-5
Member Dupont Circle Fine Art Galleries

Artists' Cooperative
Director: Randolph Michener
Cash, check, MasterCard, Visa, payment plan
Established 1975

Foundry's large space above Addision/Ripley Gallery is devoted to two solo exhibit spaces and a members' gallery, all of which offer changing exhibits featuring the works of members as well as artists around the country. Foundry sponsors regular curated and juried shows in support of good contemporary art by non-members.

MEDIA: Many of the members work in abstract styles and media, including installations. Most two- and three-dimensional media are shown, though.

STYLES: Foundry artists are especially interested in experimental work, although all contemporary styles are shown.

ARTISTS REGULARLY SHOWN: Members include Hector L. Almodovar, Brook Andrews, Monica Bacmeister (figurative, expressionist acrylic paintings), Alex Bay (whimsical sculpture), Jessica C. Damen, Anne Marie Fleming, Linda Sauerland Hendricks, Randy Michener (photographs), Betty Murchison, Nancy Salome Sanford, William Schran, Robert Tiemann, Ann Wallace, David Yerkes.

SELECTION OF NEW ARTISTS: New members are selected by majority vote when openings arise. A one-year contract starts at $80/month. Members are entitled to one solo show per year and several group shows. Members gallery-sit one or two days per month. Artists interested in joining are welcome to send slides and a resumé.

GALLERY 10 LTD.

1519 Connecticut Avenue, N.W.
Washington, DC 20036
(202)232-3326
Tuesday-Saturday 11-5
Member Dupont Circle Fine Art Galleries

Artists' Cooperative
Director: Ruth Gancie
Cash, check, MasterCard, Visa, payment plan
Established 1974

One of the best galleries in town, Gallery 10 is owned by a corporation of 10 artists, all of whom show here. However, the member-owners also curate exciting shows featuring the work of other artists; Gallery 10 has developed a reputation for being a risk-taking place that has shown new work by East Coast artists.

Gallery 10 occasionally produces a show catalog. For example, the catalog of their Tenth Anniversary exhibition in 1984 featured reproductions of the work of every artist shown, whether members or not, and an introduction by Jane Addams Allen. Allen wrote,

It's a risk-taking enterprise which puts imagination above craft and passions above good manners....What is really unusual about Gallery 10, though, is that in the course of the last decade its members haven't lost their appetite for new and raw art....They haven't let reality bludgeon them into safe decisions or self-interest distort their judgment.

MEDIA: Paintings, sculpture, photography, prints, collage, installation.

STYLES: Contemporary styles—representational through experimental.

ARTISTS REGULARLY SHOWN: 10 member-owners: Maxine Cable (visionary assemblages and installations), Noche Crist, JoAnn Crisp-Ellert, Elizabeth Friedman, Ruth Gancie, Mary McCoy, Gloria Monteiro, Jeanne O'Donnell, Emily Rose, Hildegarde van Roijen (metal sculpture).

SELECTION OF NEW ARTISTS: Member-owners meet once a month to look at artists' slides in their quest to discover interesting artists to feature in solo or group shows. They look for originality, proficiency, professionalism, and consistency. New partners are not sought at this time, although guest artists are always sought.

Bird Shrine (detail), 1985, by Maxine R. Cable. Installation, 8'x20'x8'. Photograph by F. N. Wells. Gallery 10.

Construction,
by Ann Stein.
Oil on canvas,
24"x20".
Gallery West.

GALLERY WEST

1309 King Street
Alexandria, VA 22314
(703)549-7359
Wednesday-Friday 10-4,
Saturday-Sunday 11-5

Artists' Cooperative
Director: Joan Liebman
Cash, check, payment plan
Established 1979

On the edge of Old Town Alexandria, this small, well-lit gallery offers a sophisticated mix of artwork by emerging artists in a variety of media and styles. It is a storefront gallery near the King Street Metro stop. Prices are reasonable, both for one-of-a-kinds and the small original prints which are available in a small bin.

MEDIA: Paintings, drawings, sculpture, photographs, original prints, collage.
STYLES: Run the gamut.
ARTISTS REGULARLY SHOWN: Members: Helen Brown, Max Bullock, John Clendening, Omar Dasent, Hector V. Diaz, Alicia Dobranski, Joan M. Earnhart, Claire Freeman, Judy Gallegos, Jill E. Henriod, Terrance Kuch, Joan LIebman, Pamela McDonough, Stephanie S. Ney, Gesine Noonan, Helen Ottaway, Barbara Y. Roberts, Kathleen Schall, Carole M. Shoemaker, Bonnie Shevrock, Laura Simpson, Ann Stein, Maria B. Valero.
SELECTION OF NEW ARTISTS: Jurying for new members takes place the first Monday of each month. Membership dues are $50 per month. Members must gallery sit one day each month and help prepare for one or more shows per year. Members are entitled to one three-week solo show approximately every two years.

HERNDON OLD TOWN GALLERY

720 Lynn Street
Herndon, VA 22070
(703)435-2772
Tuesday-Saturday 10-5, Sunday 12-5

Director: Lassie Corbett
Cash, check, MasterCard, Visa
Established 1985

The Herndon Old Town Gallery is housed in a renovated turn-of-the-century building. They will be opening a second gallery location in March; interested parties are invited to call for information.

Several other artists are in residence in the building, working on-site during business hours. In addition, classes are regularly offered.

MEDIA: Paintings, drawings, collage, porcelain and ceramic pieces from bowls to wall pieces, fiber, glass.

STYLES: Many styles of work are available, including traditional, representational, and architectural ornamentation. Commissions are always welcome.

ARTISTS REGULARLY SHOWN: Members include Marion Buckner, Lassie Corbett, Barbara Kennikell, Pat McIntyre, Carol Milton, Elaine Oliver, Terry Schultz, Margaret Story, Jack Ward, Maggie Waters, Darlene Watson, Marilyn Weiss.

SELECTION OF NEW ARTISTS: New members are selected when an opening arises. In the meantime, the gallery likes to include work by other artists to complement their own pieces. Artists are welcome to call for an appointment and/or more information.

Installation photograph of 1987 work by gallery artists.
Old Mill Gallery.

OLD MILL GALLERY

1696 Chain Bridge Road
at Rt. 123 entrance, Evans Farm Inn
McLean, VA 22101
(703)893-2736
Tuesday-Sunday 11-5

Artists' Cooperative
Cash, check, MasterCard, Visa
Price Range: $3-900
Established 1982

Surrounded by water, weeping willows, and geese, the Old Mill Gallery is in a beautiful, rustic stone structure which once was used as a mill. The well-lit interior of this craft artists' cooperative offers the visitor two storeys full of well-displayed, invariably well executed, and reasonably priced fine craft works.

MEDIA: Wearables include gorgeous hand-painted silk scarves, jewelry, hand-woven angora and/or wool sweaters, belts, and more. Functionals include woven linens, ceramics, baskets, wooden bowls, and more. *Objets* are available as well.

STYLES: Traditional to contemporary; well-executed.

ARTISTS REGULARLY SHOWN: Carol Cavanaugh, Judy Clark, Georgann Cullen, Barbara Dahlquist, Shannon Denny, Ann Granger, Inger Hegstad, Nancy Jemio, Nancy Johnson, Karen Miner, Amy Rondon, Barbara Ryan, Rosemary Stokes, Beth Surdut, Terry Svat, Sue Tansey, Laureen Vlaisavljevich, Betsy Wilding, Jack Zimmerman.

SELECTION OF NEW ARTISTS: Jurying for new members takes place when there is an opening. Membership dues are $20 per month. Each member must gallery-sit approximately one day per month and serve on a committee. Examples of all members' work is on display at all times; there are no solo shows. However, special shows are organized around certain themes, i.e. wearables. Artists interested in joining are encouraged to send slides and a letter of interest.

Carousel, by John Brock.
Stoneware.
Spectrum Gallery.

SPECTRUM GALLERY

1132 29th Street, N.W.
Washington, DC 20008
(202)333-0954
Tuesday-Saturday 10-5,
Sunday 1-5

Artists' Cooperative
Director: Millie Shott
Price Range: $15-2,500
Cash, check, MasterCard, Visa,
American Express, payment plan
Established 1966

A street level Georgetown gallery just off M Street, Spectrum shows a wide variety of work by area artists.

MEDIA: Paintings, works on paper, original prints, sculpture, collage, crafts, handmade paper, jewelry, and ceramics.

STYLES: Representational, impressionist; abstract, including experimental, minimalist, abstract expressionist, expressionist; surrealist. Most members are open to commissions.

ARTISTS REGULARLY SHOWN: 29 members include: Betsy Anderson, Sandra Baggette, Shirley Bounds, John Brock, John Bryans, Edythe Cardon, June Carlough, Gina Clopp, Selma Cohen, Raymond Ewing, Jeannie Garant, Ray Gesumaria, Viola Glick, Gwen Graine, Barbara Haeme, Peggy Hawley, Jill Hemriod, Dorothy Hunter, Wilma King, Margaret Kranking, Ingrid Leeds, Carol Lopatin, Lindsay Makepeace, Alice Mostoff, Tom Raneses, Doris Reis, Cora Rupp, Kate Steiger, Marjean Willett.

SELECTION OF NEW ARTISTS: Membership is based on peer review as openings become available. Membership dues are $50 per month after an initiation fee of $200. Members gallery-sit about once every three weeks, and each member is entitled to one solo show every two years. Artists interested in joining are encouraged to drop in to see the gallery and file an application of interest for the next available slot.

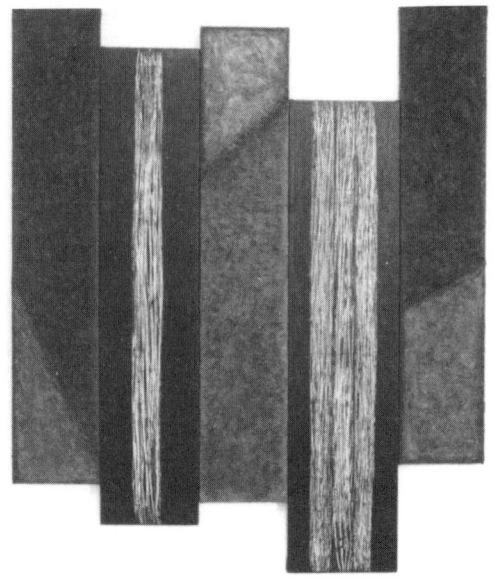

Source, by Erwin Lachman. Acrylic on canvas, five panels, 52"x43". Studio Gallery.

STUDIO GALLERY

2108 R Street, N.W.
Washington, DC 20008
(202)232-8734
Tuesday-Saturday 11-5
Member Dupont Circle Fine Art Galleries

Artists' Cooperative
Director: Kay Kaiser
Price Range: $50-3,000
Cash, check
Established 1964

This artists' cooperative is one of Washington's oldest. In the English Basement of a townhouse near Dupont Circle, it is graced by a sculpture garden in the back.

The members are committed to providing a forum for Washington area artists through sponsorship of regular invitational and juried exhibitions.

MEDIA: Paintings, works on paper, original prints, sculpture, collage, photography, mixed.

STYLES: Eclectic.

ARTISTS REGULARLY SHOWN: 28 members include: Mary Betts Anderson, Pat Barron, Pamela Brown, Ruth Cahnmann, Marcia Coppel, Joe Fitzgerald, Nancy Frankel, Rose Goding, Phyllis Henkelman, Caroline Huff, Catherine Hunt, Kay Kaiser, Ai-Wen Wei Kratz, Erwin Lachman, Jill Lion, Mary Lynch, Sue Lynch, Bodil Meleney, Margaret Paris, Lucy Pirtle, Frances Raiford, Carol Ravenal, Ingrid Rehert, Doris Rief, Ellouise Schoettler, Gresham Sykes, Lea Topping, Carol Vanderpool, Hilda Witherspoon, Ann Zahn.

SELECTION OF NEW ARTISTS: Membership is based on peer review; portfolio reviews are held monthly. Membership dues are $60/month plus an initiation fee of $60. Members must gallery sit about four times per year and serve on a committee. Members are entitled to one solo show approximately every two years. There is a continuous but changing membership show of small works in the Alcove section.

Life After Life, 1987, by Hilda Witherspoon. Acrylic on paper, 26"x40". Studio Gallery.

Spirit: The Cow, 1987, by Dona Gunther-Brown. Oil on canvas, 40"x36". Photograph by Tom Clark. Touchstone Gallery, page 84.

TOUCHSTONE GALLERY

2130 P Street, N.W.
Washington, DC 20037
(202)223-6683
Tuesday-Saturday 11-5,
Sunday 12-5
Member Dupont Circle Fine Art Galleries

Artists' Cooperative
Director: Luba Dreyer
Cash, check, MasterCard, Visa, payment plan
Price Range: $100-6,000
Established 1976

This 1,250 sq. ft. storefront gallery is located across the street from the Georgetown Omni Hotel. The gallery shows the works of members, as well as curated shows.

Touchstone also features lectures by Washington art notables, and other outreach programs for the Washington art community.

MEDIA: Paintings, works on paper, original prints, sculpture, photography, installations.

STYLES: Representational, expressionist, surrealist, abstract, abstract-expressionist, conceptual, minimalist, experimental.

ARTISTS REGULARLY SHOWN: There are about 30 members, including Altina ("people benches"), Ann Barbieri, Allene Bary-Cooper, Andrea Burchette, Aldeth S. Christy, Susan Clifford, Richard Dana, Joseph DeBor, Connie Fleres, Gretchen Friend-Jones (mixed media symbolist paintings), Dona Gunther-Brown, Marylou Hartmann, Mansoora Hasan, Leni Liftin, Glenn Moreton, Harriet Rosenbaum, Sheila Rotner, Deirdre Saunder, Charles Sawchenko, Dana Scheurer, Rima Schulkind, Thomas Scott, Frances Seeger, Laura Schwartz, Frank Smith, Judith Turim, Frank Van Riper, David Yocum, Zinnia (photographs and installations).

SELECTION OF NEW ARTISTS: Applicants are juried by current members. Artists wishing to join must submit a body of actual work and slides of previous work for peer review; a two-thirds vote is required. Members receive a solo show every two years. The annual fee is $600. Members gallery-sit one day each month.

TOWN CENTER GALLERY, INC.

Rockville Metro Center,
250 Hungerford Drive
Rockville, MD 20850
(301)424-7313
Monday-Saturday 11-4

Artists' Cooperative
Director: Barbara Leyba
Cash, check, MasterCard, Visa,
American Express, payment plan
Established 1971

Town Center Gallery has moved to a new space in the Rockville Metro Center.

MEDIA: Paintings, drawings, collage, prints of all kinds.

STYLES: Traditional, representational, impressionist, expressionist, abstract, abstract-expressionist.

ARTISTS REGULARLY SHOWN: Members include: Elizabeth Allen, Ann Blackwell, Kathy Blozan, Rober Bucklin, Ellen Burgoyne, Sally Carlson, Bernice Duvall, Yolanda Frederikse, Mary Goodwin, Jane Hill, Linda Kirvan, Barbara Leyba, Jim Masters, Liz McKelway, Eric Mohn, Eileen Nader, Barbara Nuss, Edie Pyle, Fred Rupko, Carol Vorosmarti, Opal Ward, Gertrude Wetmore, Connie Woolard.

SELECTION OF NEW ARTISTS: Jurying for new members takes place when there is an opening. Interested artists are encouraged to contact the gallery for further information.

Truman's Sentries, 1986, by Marcy Shear Wolpe. Serigraph, $25^1/2"$ x $16^1/4"$. Photograph by Joel Breger. Washington Printmakers Gallery.

WASHINGTON PRINTMAKERS GALLERY

2106 R Street, N.W.
Washington, DC 20008
(202)332-7757
Tuesday-Saturday 11-5

Artists' Cooperative
Director: Carolyn Pomponio
Manager: Sharon Celestini
Price Range: $20-500
Cash, check, MasterCard, Visa
Established 1985

This gallery is located in the English Basement level below the Anton Gallery. It is an unusual gallery in that it specializes in one medium: original hand-pulled prints.

MEDIA: Original prints, in black-and-white and color: silkscreen, etching, monotype, lithograph, aquatint, collagraph, woodcut, linocut. Some pieces incorporate elements of collage and handmade paper; some pieces utilize multiple plates.

STYLES: Run the gamut.

ARTISTS REGULARLY SHOWN: 25 members include: P. Barringer, P. Wedd-Brown, B. Caples, G. Chung, C. Clark, S. De Quadros, M. French, C. Grace, L. Huff, C. Huffman, P. Jakobsberg, K. Kelly, J. M. Linsley, E. G. Ochs, M. Osher, S. Pearcy, C. Pomponio, G. Roberts, M. Ross, D. Schindler, D. Stratto, T. Svat, N. Tran, S. Wasko-Flood, M. Shear-Wolpe.

SELECTION OF NEW ARTISTS: New members are juried by current members. Artists wishing to join are welcome to send a letter with slides or call for an appointment.

Functional

JACKIE CHALKLEY (Two locations)

3301 New Mexico Avenue, N.W.
Washington, DC 20016
(202)686-8882
Monday-Saturday 10-5:30
Established 1978
Owner: Jackie Chalkley
Director: Margaret Sohn

1455 Pennsylvania Avenue, N.W., Suite 130
Washington, DC 20004
(202)638-3060
Monday-Saturday 10-7
Established 1986
Director: Lisa David
Cash, check, MasterCard, Visa,
American Express, payment plans

In January of 1986, Jackie Chalkley, a potter, announced the opening of her new store adjacent to the newly restored Willard Hotel. The 1,100 sq. ft. space, which was designed by John Vorhes and Milo Hoots, is a work of art in itself; it was named Best Commercial Design of 1986 by the American Society of Interior Designers. Four terra cotta columns by ceramic artist Bennett Bean stand in the center of the high-ceilinged atrium; a black marble fountain is in front of the store.

Both Chalkley galleries carry one-of-a-kind and limited edition wearable art, and functional and decorative craft pieces. Regular one-person and group exhibitions highlight new work.

MEDIA: Hand-made, unique or limited edition, decorative and wearable arts: Fiber, glass, wood, clay, metal, paper.

STYLES: Anything that is well-designed and well-crafted.

ARTISTS REGULARLY SHOWN: The work of over 400 artists and designers is available, including: Solveig Cox, Mary George Kronstadt, Ron Splude (silk jacquard belts and scarves), Will Richards, Tim Harding, Taylor Backes, Steve Smyers.

SELECTION OF NEW ARTISTS: Artists are welcome to send a letter with slides and resumé. New artists are chosen based primarily on saleability, originality and proficiency, and looks which suit the style of the store.

GALLERY BY LEE

767 South 23rd Street
Arlington, VA 22202
(703)979-4314
Tuesday-Saturday 11-6

Owner/Directors: Cliff and Holly Lee
Price Range: $15-5,000
Cash, check, MasterCard, Visa, payment plan
Established 1977

Holly Lee is a jeweler who works with semiprecious stones; her work is highly original. Often, designs come to her in dreams. Cliff Lee, once a medical student, is a potter who uses Celadon, Imperial Yellow, and other fine glazes.

The Lees opened their gallery to market their own work as well as work by other artists.

MEDIA: Porcelain, jewelry, small abstract sculpture.

STYLES: Well-crafted original designs.

ARTISTS REGULARLY SHOWN: The Lees frequently invite guest artists to show there, but no one is represented *per sé*.

SELECTION OF NEW ARTISTS: The Lees prefer to discover artists themselves.

MOGUL GALLERY
[See Color Plate after page 64]

2114 R Street, N.W.
Washington, DC 20008
(202)328-8222
Tuesday-Saturday 12-6

Owner/Director: Franklin Parrasch
Cash, check, American Express, payment plan
Established 1986

Mogul Gallery, in a townhouse at the corner of Florida and R, deals in museum-quality wood furniture by contemporary artists. The work here is all one-of-a-kind. Although the furniture is functional, the designs are unique and always full of surprises.

Some of the surfaces look like marble or metal, but they are actually wood.

Treated like fine sculpture, the furniture art here is displayed on pedestals.

MEDIA: Original hand-crafted wood furniture.

STYLES: Very unusual; original contemporary designs; always well crafted. Commissions can be arranged.

ARTISTS REGULARLY SHOWN: The furniture work of over 40 artists is available at Mogul, including work by Peter S. Dean, Tage Frid, George Gordon, Kristina Madsen, Jere Osgood, Steve Pemberton, Mitch Ryerson, Rosanne Somerson, Stephen Whitney, and Barry Yavener.

SELECTION OF NEW ARTISTS: Artists may send slides with a resumé and recommendations. They may be selected based on originality, proficiency of technique, and professional experience.

MOON, BLOSSOMS AND SNOW

225 Pennsylvania Avenue, S.E.
Washington, DC 20003
(202)543-8181
Monday-Friday 11-6, Saturday 10-5

Owner: Sharon McCarthy
Director: Linda McLain
Cash, check, MasterCard, Visa, American Express
Established 1977

Nee Mamori, this gallery was re-named in 1984; as the new name may suggest, there is a Japanese feeling to much of the work here, although it is generally American. The 1,200 sq. ft. space presents the work of about 300 contemporary American artists working in fine craft media.

MEDIA: Two- and three-dimensional crafts; functional, wearable, and decorative. Fiber, jewelry, ceramics, glass, wood, paper, and mixed.

STYLES: Well-crafted.

ARTISTS REGULARLY SHOWN: Alex & Noble (fabric jewelry, bags, garments); Nancy Lyons (hand-woven and -constructed clothing); Nancy Frank (lacquered wood cuff bracelets); Harvey Greenwald (leather handbags and briefcases); Hilary Gifford (silk garments).

SELECTION OF NEW ARTISTS: Artists may send slides with a resumé and recommendations. They may be selected based on technique, saleability, and originality.

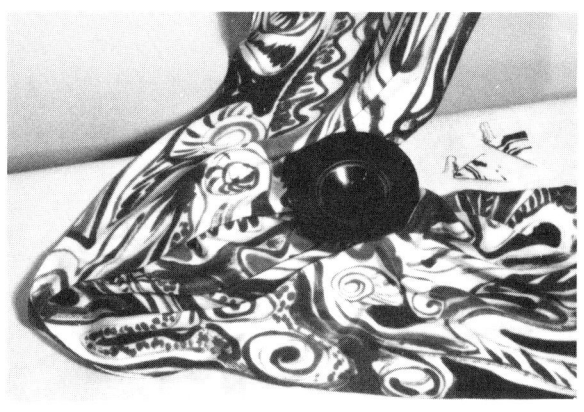

Installation photograph of 1987 works:
silk painting by Marilyn Morris,
porcelain bowl and earrings
by Tui Morse.
Marilyn Morris Gallery.

MARILYN MORRIS FINE ARTS

1201 31st Street, N.W.
Washington, DC 20007
(202)333-2888
Monday-Saturday 11-6

Owner/Director: Marilyn Morris
Price Range: $50-2,500
Cash, check, MasterCard, Visa
Established 1986

Marilyn Morris, an artist herself, produces paintings and hand-painted silk. She opened her small Georgetown gallery to market her own work as well as fine craft works by other artists. A second space, open at another location by appointment, has larger artworks on hand.

Special events are held, such as poetry readings and musical performances.

MEDIA: Paintings, drawings, sculpture, photography, original prints, collage, wearables, artists' books/paper, porcelain, ceramics, fiber.

STYLES: A wide variety of styles from traditional to abstract. Commissions can be arranged.

ARTISTS REGULARLY SHOWN: Marian Fountain (bronzes), Barbie Sadori (beadwork), Gordon Nash (blown glass).

SELECTION OF NEW ARTISTS: Artists are welcome to phone for an appointment to show slides of larger works, or samples of smaller pieces. Artists are chosen based on originality and proficiency of technique.

OLD MILL GALLERY

Please refer to the preceding chapter, Cooperative Galleries.

ORIGINAL ACCENTS

Village Centre
766 Walker Road
Great Falls, VA 22066
(703)759-6749
Monday-Saturday 10-5

Owner/Directors: Jill Charron,
Ann Dove, Gerd Spangenburg
Price Range: $15-1,000
Cash, check, MasterCard, Visa
Established 1983

This handsome gallery showcases a wide variety of beautifully crafted objects in a well-lit and spacious setting.

MEDIA: Wearables, architectural ("stained") glass, ceramics, carved wood.

STYLES: Original designs, mostly conservative styles.

ARTISTS REGULARLY SHOWN: Gary Upton (Swedish door harps), Janice Midkiff (clay and beaded jewelry), Ken Pellar (glass panels).

SELECTION OF NEW ARTISTS: Artists may call for an appointment. S/he may be invited to send slides, or to come in with samples.

PIRJO

655 15th Street, N.W.
Washington, DC 20005
(202)393-1390
Monday-Friday 10:30-6,
Saturday 12-5

Owner/Director: Pirjo Jaffe
Price Range: $30-500
Cash, check, MasterCard, Visa,
American Express
Established 1986

Proprietor Pirjo Jaffe, originally from Finland, is a fiber artist. Along with ready-mades, Pirjo carries a fine stock of hand-crafted wearables. Jewelry is made by primarily American artists, and the clothing is generally made by Finnish artists.

MEDIA: Wearable art.

STYLES: Original designs, mostly traditional Finnish techniques.

ARTISTS REGULARLY SHOWN: Helen Sharp (knitted, brilliantly colored sweaters and jackets); Sirkka Kononen (sweaters knitted in folk patterns from handspun wool).

SELECTION OF NEW ARTISTS: Artists may send slides with a resumé and recommendations. They may be selected based on technique, saleability, and originality.

SANSAR

4200 Wisconsin Avenue, N.W.
Tenley Mall
Washington, DC 20016
(202)244-4448
Tuesday-Saturday 10-6 (Wednesday until 9)

Owner/Director: Veena Singh
Co-Director: Kathleen Gilder
Cash, check, MasterCard, Visa,
American Express, payment plan
Established 1981

Veena Singh is a furniture designer herself. Sansar specializes in contemporary American craft furniture. However, Singh has just begun to handle contemporary works on paper and fine craft pieces from around the world as well.

Interior design and furniture restoration services are also offered.

MEDIA: Contemporary American handmade furniture; contemporary works on paper; craft works in media including ceramics, glass, jewelry; accessories from India and Bali; furniture, including French Deco.

STYLES: Generally functional fine craft pieces.

ARTISTS REGULARLY SHOWN: Furniture designers: Ronnie Puckett, Robert Kowalski, Mark Sfirri, Bob March, Lorna Secrest, John C. Harvey, Chris Weiland, John Clark. Other artists: David Fry (turned bowls of burled wood), Mary Angus (glass), Amy Sarner (airbrushed glazed ceramics).

SELECTION OF NEW ARTISTS: Singh prefers to discover artists herself. She looks for consistency, proficiency of technique, originality, and saleability.

VENI VIDI VICI

$3061^1/2$ M Street, N.W.
Second Floor
Washington, DC 20007
(202)333-8424
Monday-Saturday 10-5:30

Owners: Nicole Chapman
and Geneva Haag
Price Range: $10-3,000
Cash, check, MasterCard, Visa,
American Express, payment plan
Established 1986

The gallery specializes in wearable art: jewelry, and original fiber art *cum* clothing. Some of the most striking original wearables in town are available here.

They also operate a wholesale showroom.

In February 1988, Veni Vidi Vici will be moving to a new space between Old Georgetown and Wisconsin Avenues. The address will be 4902 Fairmont Avenue, Bethesda, Maryland 20814.

MEDIA: Wearables. Fiber: woven, painted, felted, etc.). Jewelry: precious and other metals, ivory, wood, fiber, found. A small selection of fine crafts is also on hand.

STYLES: Conservative to way-out, but always highly original.

ARTISTS REGULARLY SHOWN: Over 100 artists include: Terry Phillips, and Luba Taubvertzel (hand-painted silk garments); Cynthia Boyer (felted garments); Debra Koval (jewelry made of high-tech found, i.e. TV, parts); Gail Singer and Elise Stigliano (leather accessories); Pat Perito (silver jewelry); Teresa Cole (unique bead work); Harriet Moss (handwoven garments); Joyce Edwards (hand knitted garments).

SELECTION OF NEW ARTISTS: Artists may phone for an appointment to show samples. Mostly Washington artists are represented, but a few international craft people round out the list. New artists are selected based on originality, technique, and saleability.

VO GALERIE

2000 Pennsylvania Avenue, N.W.
Washington, DC 20006
(202)293-0249
Monday-Friday 10-7, Saturday 10-6

Owner/Director: Joke Van Ommen
Cash, check, MasterCard, Visa,
American Express, payment plan
Established 1984

Joke (pronounced Yoke) van Ommen, a native of Holland, is a master goldsmith. She shows jewelry work by contemporary, even avant garde, European jeweler/artists. About 20 percent of the artists are American.

MEDIA: Anything which translates into wearable jewelry.

STYLES: Any well-crafted style. Conservative to highly abstract.

ARTISTS REGULARLY SHOWN: Original jewelry by about 50 artists is regularly on display. Artists include: Andrea Halmschlager (whimsical papier maché); Herman Hermsen; Ronnie Lowensteyn (position-it-yourself brooches); Esther Knobel (flat articulated metal pieces); Caroline Broadhead; Pavel Opocensky (ivory); Marjorie Schick; Giampaolo Babetto.

SELECTION OF NEW ARTISTS: Jewelry artists interested in representation may phone for an appointment to show samples, or send a letter with slides, resumé, and perhaps a sample.

Multiples and More

ART UNLIMITED

6715 Backlick Road
Springfield, VA 22150
(703)569-4444
Monday-Saturday 10-6 (Thursday 10-8)

Owner/Directors: Jeff and Pamela Fahrner
Price Range: $125-1,000
Cash, check, MasterCard, Visa,
American Express, payment plan

Although a huge bin at Art Unlimited contains "original oil paintings for $28 and up," there are a few really fine drawings and limited edition prints available here. The facility is very large, and a variety of two-dimensional work is on display.

Art Unlimited offers custom framing services.

MEDIA: Prints (from originals to unsigned offsets), drawings, paintings.

STYLES: Impressionist, representational, naive, folk, western, nautical.

ARTISTS REGULARLY SHOWN: 75, including Mel Hunter (large color lithographs, dramatic nature subjects), Robert Bateman.

SELECTION OF NEW ARTISTS: Artists are chosen based primarily on proficiency of technique, originality of content, and saleability. Artists may send a letter of interest or call for an appointment; the directors wish to see original work.

VIRGINIA BADER FINE ARTS LIMITED

1305 King Street
Alexandria, VA 22314
(703)548-4440, (800)233-0345 outside Virginia
Monday-Saturday 10-5

Owner: Virginia Bader
Director: Sandra Sterne
Price Range: $100-10,000
Cash, check, MasterCard, Visa
Established 1977

Located less than 10 minutes from National Airport, this is the only gallery in the area specializing in aviation art.

The artists whose work is available here are some of the best in the field of aviation art. Some of them have been given solo shows at the National Air and Space Museum, others have work on permanent exhibit there in the form of murals and illustrations.

Aircraft from balloons and taildraggers to World War II and the most modern fighter planes are depicted. Some of the pieces also feature the signatures of the pilots who flew the plane(s) in a particular image. The gallery sponsors Meet-the-Pilot receptions as well as Meet-the-Artist openings.

MEDIA: Medium- to large-edition prints as well as original oils are available. Commissions can be arranged.

STYLES: Realist.

ARTISTS REGULARLY SHOWN: Bill Phillips, Robert Taylor, Keith Ferris, Frank Wootten, James Dietz.

SELECTION OF NEW ARTISTS: Artists working in the appropriate subject matter may send photographs of their work or a sample lithograph.

BISHOP'S GALLERY

3300 M Street, N.W.
Washington, DC 20007
(202)333-7701
Tuesday-Sunday 11-6

Owners: John Bishop; Andrew Mercer;
Bob Pass; and JoAnn Pass
Cash, check, MasterCard, Visa,
American Express, payment plan
Established 1987

Affiliated with galleries of the same name in Scottsdale, LaJolla, and San Diego, Bishop's Gallery handles a generous mix of contemporary work. This plush, beautifully lit gallery offers a fair number of one-of-a-kind artworks along with multiples.
MEDIA: Paintings, drawings, sculpture, wearables, original prints, collage, offsets.
STYLES: Traditional, representational, abstract, naive, oriental, impressionist, abstract-expressionist.
ARTISTS REGULARLY SHOWN: Erté, Miro, Jiang, He Neng, Tamayo, Frederick Hart (figurative acrylic sculpture), Yamagata, Neiman, Alvar.
SELECTION OF NEW ARTISTS: Artists are welcome to send slides and a resumé.

DAMON GALLERIES, LTD.

220 Maple Avenue W.
Vienna, VA 22180
(703)938-7000
Monday-Saturday 10-6 (Thursday 10-8)

Owner/Director: Shirley S. Damon
Cash, check, MasterCard, Visa,
American Express, payment plan
Established 1974

Damon Galleries handles paintings, drawings, and original prints, along with medium- to large-edition offsets.
This gallery also offers custom framing services.
MEDIA: Paintings, drawings, collage, prints.
STYLES: Contemporary but generally representational.
ARTISTS REGULARLY SHOWN: Charles Harper, Ray Harm, Florine Gompf, Jean Victor, Alan Hunt, Jim Harrison, Randy Owens, Melinda Harleman, Kathleen Cantin (intricate color intaglio etchings), Virgil Thrasher.
SELECTION OF NEW ARTISTS: Artists may send a letter with recommendations, a resumé, and slides, or may phone for an appointment. Artists are chosen based primarily on proficiency of technique, originality, and saleability.

GALLERIE JULIAN (Two locations)

[See Color Plate after page 64]

506 King Street
Alexandria, VA 22314
(703)548-6203
Monday-Saturday 10-6, Sunday 12-6

1055 Thomas Jefferson Street, N.W.
Washington, DC 20007
(202)333-5162
Owner/Director: T. T. Nieh
Cash, check, MasterCard, Visa, American Express, lease/purchase plan, payment plan
Established 1981

Both Julians are attractive, large galleries in new buildings—amazing considering they are in historic areas: Old Town Alexandria, and near the Canal in Georgetown.

T. T. Nieh says Julian was opened "to provide a showplace for fine art published and distributed by its parent company, T. T. Nieh Publishing, as well as to exhibit unique works of art by selected great and 'yet-to-be-great' living European and American artists."

Gallerie Julian also features special events such as classical concerts given by solo pianists and small chamber groups.

MEDIA: Paintings, drawings, sculpture, photography, original prints, artists' books/paper, wearables.

STYLES: Impressionist, expressionist, abstract, abstract-expressionist, oriental.

ARTISTS REGULARLY SHOWN: More than 50, including: Pang Tseng-Ying, Uzilevsky, Secunda, John Swanson (serigraphs with musical and Biblical imagery).

SELECTION OF NEW ARTISTS: The director of Gallerie Julian is not currently interested in reviewing portfolios.

GEORGETOWN FINE ARTS

3222 M Street, N.W.
Washington, DC 20007
(202)342-9654
Monday-Friday 10-9, Saturday 10-7,
Sunday 12-6

Owner/Director: Peggy Wollins
Price Range: $400-10,000
Cash, check, MasterCard, Visa, American Express, payment plan
Established 1981

Georgetown Fine Arts works primarily with contemporary graphics in editions of all sizes.

However, a special feature here is that once a year they throw a celebrity-artist opening to kick off an exhibit by that artist. Stars who have shown their work at Georgetown Fine Arts include Tony Bennett and the late John Lennon.

MEDIA: Prints, drawings, paintings.

STYLES: Abstract to representational.

ARTISTS REGULARLY SHOWN: Besides Bennett and Lennon: Thomas McKnight, Erté, Joanna Zjawinska, Harold Altman.

SELECTION OF NEW ARTISTS: Artists are welcome to send a letter with slides and resumé, or call for an appointment.

HENSLEY GALLERY

1311 King Street
Alexandria, VA 22314
(703)836-1010
Tuesday-Saturday 10-5

Owner/Director: Jim Hamilton
Cash, check, MasterCard, Visa, payment plan
Established 1978

One-of-a-kind pieces including paintings, drawings, and signed original prints are available, as well as signed offsets and posters.

Custom framing services are offered.

MEDIA: Paintings, pastels, photography, prints (original, signed offsets, and unsigned offsets).

STYLES: Traditional, abstract, naive.

ARTISTS REGULARLY SHOWN: Millie Bennett (American primitive; oil paintings and prints); Kugler (abstract oil paintings).

SELECTION OF NEW ARTISTS: Hensley Gallery is not currently reviewing portfolios.

IMAGES INTERNATIONAL

3 Bethesda Metro Center
Bethesda, MD 20814
(301)654-3938
Monday-Saturday 10-6

Owner: Beverly A. Hill
Director: Phillip Lamb
Cash, check, MasterCard, Visa, American Express, payment plan
Established 1985

Images International, affiliated with Images International of Hawaii, is located in the Plaza level of the Atrium Building. Before being a gallery owner, Beverly Hill was a professional ballroom dancer. Much of the work has the sweeping lines of a dancer in motion.

Images International is concerned with "creating the appropriate art 'image' for the home, executive suite, corporate office, bank, restaurant, or hospital." One interesting feature is the one-year exchange policy. Other services offered include interior image design, custom framing, delivery, and installation.

MEDIA: Paintings, drawings, sculpture (bronze and lucite), prints of large and small editions, mixed, artists' books and paper.

STYLES: Representational, surrealist, oriental, impressionist, abstract.

ARTISTS REGULARLY SHOWN: Elba Alvarez; Laurie Fields; John Cosby; Doug Eisman; Makk family (Americo, Eva, A.B.); Hisashi Otsuka; Peter Howard; Adolf Sehring; Andrea Smith.

SELECTION OF NEW ARTISTS: Artists are welcome to send slides and a resumé, drop in with same, or call for an appointment. Shows are scheduled several months ahead of time.

P & C ART, INC. (Four locations)

1. 3301 M Street, N.W.
Washington, DC 20007
(202)965-4630
Opening soon
3. 825 E. Rockville Pike
Rockville, MD 20852
(301)251-0360
Monday-Saturday 10-7, Sunday 12:30-5
Cash, check, MasterCard, Visa, American Express

2. 2400 Wisconsin Avenue, N.W.
Washington, DC 20007
(202)965-2485
Tuesday-Saturday 10-7, Sunday 12:30-6
4. 2817 Dorr Avenue, Unit D
Fairfax, VA 22031
(703)698-9350
By appointment
President: Peter Nee

The nicely appointed P&C galleries carry primarily limited- to large-edition prints by a number of artists, and some limited edition sculpture by Erté.

P&C offers custom framing services, headquartered at their Fairfax location which is also known as Capital Art & Framing. This particular branch of P&C is also a wholesale showroom for designers and art consultants; the 4,000 square foot facility handles a special line of graphics for resale to the trade.

MEDIA: Medium- to large-edition prints as well as original oils are available. Commissions can be arranged.

STYLES: Abstract, representational, figurative, Art Deco.

ARTISTS REGULARLY SHOWN: Printmakers represented include Thomas McKnight, Graciela Boulanger, Erté, Jiang Tie-Feng, Michel Delacroix, Kipniss, and Behrens.

SELECTION OF NEW ARTISTS: P&C handles work by major art publishers; hence, Peter Nee is not interested in reviewing portfolios at this time.

PAVO REAL

Georgetown Park
3222 M Street, N.W.
Washington, DC 20007
(202)338-3128
Monday-Friday 10-9, Saturday 10-7,
 Sunday 12-6

Owner: Tom J. Brush
Director: Ann Rushforth Semko
Price Range: $175-5,000
Cash, check, MasterCard, Visa,
American Express, payment plan
Established 1980

Pavo Real (pronounced PAH-vo re-AHL) is affiliated with four other galleries of the same name in New York, Chicago, Boston, and Boca Raton.

The interior of this gallery is very unusual—because of some of the artwork carried, it has a fantastic, surreal jungle feeling, like getting lost in a Rousseau painting.

This gallery handles a variety of work; much of it is multiple, but the multiples here are in three-dimensional media. Some interesting one-of-a-kind works are available here as well.

MEDIA: Bronze, sheet metal, ceramic, papier maché, prints.

STYLES: Traditional, representational, surrealist, naive, folk.

ARTISTS REGULARLY SHOWN: Loet Vanderveen, Randy Puckett, Sergio Bustamante.

SELECTION OF NEW ARTISTS: Artists are met with after a personal recommendation from a colleague known to the gallery.

PRINCE ROYAL GALLERY

204 South Royal Street
Alexandria, VA 22314
(703)548-5151
Tuesday-Saturday 11-5, Sunday 1-5,
Monday 11-5 April-September

Owners: John and Peg Byers
Directors: Polly Doolin, Chris Walker
Price Range: $20-8,000
Cash, check, MasterCard, Visa
Established 1976

Prince Royal Gallery is a huge, high-ceilinged, light-filled gallery in a second-story space which once was a ballroom. It is in what used to be the Concordia Hotel in Old Town, at the corner of Prince and Royal Streets. In a way, it is more like a loft apartment/practice studio a dancer might have than a ballroom, reached by climbing a narrow stairway, plants filling the upper hall, an old kitchen visible upon entering the gallery. But once inside, there is a tremendously large gallery. Much of the work here is good one-of-a-kind work, and a large variety is available.

MEDIA: Paintings, drawings, sculpture, prints (signed originals, signed offsets, unsigned offsets).

STYLES: Representational, impressionist, naive, oriental.

ARTISTS REGULARLY SHOWN: Paul Wegner (bronze sculpture), Ralph Smith (watercolor landscapes), Kenneth Koskela (whimsical prints and watercolors; illustrative, humorous, and surrealistic), Rosemary Sandweg (oils of the Shenandoah Valley), the Hennesy family (representational oil paintings; landscapes and nauticals), P. Buckley Moss.

SELECTION OF NEW ARTISTS: Artists may drop in with slides and originals, phone for an appointment, or send a letter with slides. New artists are selected based on saleability, technique, and originality.

UPTOWN ARTS

2116 18th Street, N.W.
Washington, DC 20009
(202)387-6555
Tuesday-Saturday, 10:30-7,
Sunday 12-4

Owner: John Keegel
Director: Edward Levine
Cash, check, MasterCard, Visa,
American Express, payment plan
Established 1984

John Keegel says, "We like to carry affordable art for new and established collectors." Custom framing services are also offered.

MEDIA: Paintings, works on paper, original prints and signed offsets, collage, crafts. Two sections of the gallery are reserved for glass works and pottery.

STYLES: Traditional, representational, impressionist, abstract, expressionist, abstract expressionist, architectural, western, oriental.

ARTISTS REGULARLY SHOWN: About 40 artists are shown in a given year. Some of the artists represented include: Eric Suto, Antonio Peticov, John Zottu, Nancy Hagin, John Kiraly, Anne Raskin, M. Lambert, G. S. Gordon, David Schneuer.

SELECTION OF NEW ARTISTS: Artists interested in representation may phone for an appointment to show the portfolio, or send slides and a resumé. Criteria for the selection of new artists include proficiency of technique, saleability, and consistency in work.

GALLERIES SHOWING ART OF HISTORIC AND/OR ETHNIC SIGNIFICANCE

Commercial/Historical
Commercial/Art of Other Cultures, All Time Periods

Historical

ADAMS DAVIDSON GALLERIES
[See Color Plate after page 64]

3233 P Street, N.W.
Washington, DC 20007
(202)965-3800
Tuesday-Friday 10-5, Saturday 12-6
Member Washington Art Dealers Association,
  American Society of Appraisers

Owner: Ted Cooper
Director: Philip Carll
Cash, check, payment plan
Established 1965

Adams Davidson deals primarily in museum-quality 19th century American and occasionally European Old Master paintings and drawings.

Ted Cooper was schooled as an art historian and later as an appraiser. Both skills have enabled him to discover and procure some of the best paintings available outside of museums. In fact, sometimes museums are clients.

At any given time, works at the gallery may be representative of the Hudson River, American Impressionist, Luminist, The Eight, and other period schools. Thomas Cole, Frederic Church, Winslow Homer, Childe Hassam, Albert Bierstadt, William Bradford, Jasper Francis Cropsey, John Frederick Kensett, Alfred Thompson Bricher, John Henry Twachtman, John Singer Sargent, Worthington Whittredge, Thomas Eakins, Maurice Prendergast, and other masters' works become available here, often in the form of first-quality but works. An occasional European Old Master work turns up here as well.

A guarantee of authenticity and complete provenance is provided with every piece.

As an expert and lecturer on the valuation of American art, Cooper is also eminently qualified to provide clients with opinions, authentications, and appraisals of 19th century American art. Conservation and framing services can be arranged. Finally, gallery staff can assist in all phases of the building of collections.

Adams Davidson is located in a charming three-story townhouse in Georgetown, just off Wisconsin Avenue.

ATLANTIC GALLERY

Please refer to the Contemporary Galleries chapter. Although art shown here is very traditional in manner, it generally has been executed by contemporary living artists.

BARNES GALLERY

222 South Washington Street
Alexandria, VA 22314
(703)548-8008
Tuesday-Saturday 11-6

Owner/Directors: Jim Barnes
and Gary Eyler
Price range: $20-5,000
Cash, check, MasterCard, Visa
Established 1972

Located on the street level of a historic townhouse above their conservation/restoration workshop, the Barnes Gallery carries paintings and prints, as well as maps, manuscripts, and other historical documents.

Representative paintings include portraits, genres, nauticals, and landscapes. Two bins are full of prints: florals, wildlife, hunt scenes, opera posters, printed political cartoons by Nast from old *Harper's* magazines, and European and American city scenes including prints of Washington.

Museum-quality framing services are available.

BETHESDA ART GALLERY

P.O. Box 722
Glen Echo, MD 20812
(301)656-6665
By appointment only

Owners: Betty and Douglas Duffy
Director: Betty Minor Duffy
Price Range: $200-20,000
Cash, check
Established 1975

Bethesda Art Gallery deals exclusively in American prints dated 1900-1950. Work by over 100 20th century American master printmakers can be found here, including George Bellows, Thomas Hart Benton, Howard Cook, Edward Hopper, Childe Hassam, Walt Kuhn, John Sloan, Grant Wood, Rockwell Kent, Raphael Soyer, John Stuart Curry, Louis Lozowick, and many others. Many of these artists participated in the WPA arts projects during the '30's. Occasionally prints by living American artists like Isabel Bishop and Jonathan Meader are available.

Bethesda Art Gallery provides documentation and acid-free mats with purchases.

CALVERT GALLERY

2500 Calvert Street, N.W.
Washington, DC 20008
(in the Omni Shoreham Hotel)
(202)387-8833
10-5 Monday-Friday and
 by appointment

Owners: Peter Colosante and Maureen Taylor
Directors: Peter and Diane Colosante
Price Range: $1,000 up
Cash, check, payment plan
Established 1973

Calvert Gallery, located just off the lobby in the Shoreham Hotel, deals in fine art and antiques including 18th and 19th century furniture and paintings, porcelains sometimes of greater antiquity, and other collectibles. In addition the Calvert collection offers some contemporary art by U.S., South American, European and Middle Eastern artists.

Coursing II, 1929, by Louis Icart. Etching and drypoint, $15^1/2"\text{x}26"$.
Cherub Gallery.

CHERUB GALLERY

2918 M Street, N.W.
Washington, DC 20007
(202)337-2224
Monday-Saturday 11-6, Sunday 12-5

Owner/Director: P. Bruce Marine
Cash, check, MasterCard, Visa,
American Express
Established 1977

In the heart of Georgetown, the Cherub Gallery specializes in Art Deco artwork in the forms of oil paintings, drawings, sculpture, and original prints. Authenticity is guaranteed.

Cherub is best known as being a Louis Icart gallery, specializing in his drawings, prints and paintings in erotic and other thematic areas. However, also available are prints by Erté, drawings by Charles Dana Gibson, and glass works by René Lalique and Emile Gallé.

GALLERY LAFAYETTE

612 Duke Street
Alexandria, VA 22314
(703)548-5266
10-5 Tuesday-Saturday
  and by appointment

Owner/Director: Alyce B. Gambal
Cash, check, MasterCard, Visa,
payment plan
Established 1982

Gallery Lafayette is a cozy gallery in a two-story historic townhouse in Old Town. They often have a fire going in the winter time. Lafayette handles European and American paintings and prints dating from the 18th century through the present. Portraits, landscapes, still life, botanicals, book illustrations, genre, and traditional hunt and nautical scenes are well-represented. Artists, some of whom are living, include Stobart, Back, Cross, Barber, Audubon, Gould, Herring, Macleod, and Gilbert.

Museum-quality framing services are offered, as well as appraisal services. Paintings can be delivered to your home on a trial basis.

Contemporary artists interested in representation may phone for an appointment.

GEORGETOWN GALLERY OF ART

3235 P Street, N.W.
Washington, DC 20007
(202)333-6308
Tuesday-Saturday 11-6

Owners: Beverly and Emanuel Silberstein
Director: Emanuel Silberstein
Cash, check, payment plan
Established 1957

A half-block off Wisconsin Avenue on the Key Bridge side, the Georgetown Gallery of Art occupies the first floor of a Victorian row house.

Currently the owners specialize in the sculpture and graphics of Henry Moore. They also show work by other artists from Europe and America: oils, pastels, drawings, sculpture and original prints in traditional, representational, naive, experimental and abstract styles. About 12 other artists are shown regularly, including Leonard Baskin, Marc Chagall, and Diego Rivera. Authenticity is guaranteed.

Although the focus of Georgetown Gallery of Art is on showing artwork posthumously, living artists are sometimes selected for exhibition. Artists are welcome to send slides with a resumé and recommendations.

GUARISCO GALLERY

2828 Pennsylvania Avenue, N.W.
Washington, DC 20007
(202)333-8533
Monday-Friday 10-5:30,
Saturday 12-5

Directors: Laura Guarisco and Jane Studabaker
Cash, check, MasterCard, Visa,
American Express
Established 1981

Guarisco Gallery is adjacent to the Four Seasons Hotel, just off a brick courtyard. Guarisco specializes in 19th century, and occasional early 20th century, European and American paintings. Oils and watercolors are represented, in traditional academic styles, with impressionism being one of the bolder styles represented.

Besides still life, landscape and genre paintings, Guarisco Gallery sub-specializes in British marine paintings.

Representative works include paintings by Peter Monamy, Thomas Butterworth, Thomas Whitcombe, Thomas Luny, Isaac Sailmaker, Montague Dawson. American artists include William Sonntag, Wilson Irvine, John Dolph.

JANE HASLEM GALLERY

Please see the Contemporary Galleries section.

HOM GALLERY

2103 O Street, N.W.
Washington, DC 20037
(202)466-4076
Tuesday-Saturday 11-5
Member Art Dealers Association of America
and Dupont Circle Fine Art Galleries

Owner/Director: Jem Hom
Price Range: $500 up
Cash, check, payment plan
Established 1965

The Hom Gallery primarily handles prints, paintings and sculpture by 19th and 20th century European and American masters, including: Benton, Degas, Kollwitz, Pissarro, Prendergast, Sloan, Toulouse-Lautrec, Wood. In 1983, Hom also established a department dealing in Old Master prints, including Rembrandt and Durer. Authenticity is guaranteed.

Jem Hom says he is "always interested in purchasing or arranging the sale of fine works of art, in all media—either large collections or single items of Old Masters as well as artists of the late 19th and early 20th centuries."

In addition, Hom represents a few living artists and always has on hand examples of their current work. Jacob Kainen (prints and other works on paper) and Mark Leighauser (prints, drawings, paintings), Robert Bates, and Leonard Cave are among them. Artists interested in representation may send slides and a resumé.

KING STREET ANTIQUES

1015 King Street
Alexandria, VA 22314
(703)549-0883
Tuesday-Sunday 12-6

Owner/Director: Douglas Ritter
Price Range: $500-3,000
Cash, check, MasterCard, Visa,
payment plan
Established 1985

Housed in a two-story row house on the edge of Old Town, King Street Antiques carries English sporting paintings, drawings, and prints, along with 18th and 19th century New England primitive, to Classical Revival style, American furniture.

Equestrian art is a specialty here. Several good to excellent works are always on hand, ranging from c. 1825 oil paintings by David Dalby of York, to exquisitely executed miniature paintings on tin by an unknown European artist. The artwork is well-displayed, with ample lighting and viewing room.

Also available occasionally are seascapes and naive paintings.

Innocent Spring, mid- to late-1800's, by Edward Taylor. Watercolor, 15^1/2"x13". Patricia Kleinman, R.I.B.A. Gallery.

PATRICIA KLEINMAN R.I.B.A. GALLERY

2918 M Street, N.W.
Second floor
Washington, DC 20007
(202)337-0587
Tuesday-Saturday 11-6

Owner/Director: Patricia Kleinman
Price Range: $100-4,000
Cash, check, MasterCard, Visa,
American Express, payment plan
Established 1984

Patricia Kleinman R.I.B.A Gallery is on the second floor of the Georgetown Antique Center. Patricia Kleinman is British, and she is an architect—R.I.B.A. stands for Royal Institute of British Architects.

Kleinman deals primarily in 18th through 20th century English watercolors. All attributions are fully guaranteed: "money back and a box of Godiva chocolates" if they are wrong. She is happy to meet clients by appointment if they cannot come in during regular hours. And she likes to deal in the affordable; she is not hesitant about showing "works by good amateurs" along with the pieces she considers to be "better."

The exhibit is always changing, with about 65 paintings on display at any time. Most pieces are conservation and French matted. If not, they are listed "framed as bought."

Also worthy of note, Kleinman will sometimes buy old English watercolors if they are in good condition and signed.

LIROS GALLERY INC.

626 N. Washington Street
Alexandria, VA 22314
(703)549-7881
Monday-Friday 9-5:30, Saturday 10-4

Owner/Directors: Serge Liros
and Karen Wesley
Cash, check, MasterCard, Visa,
American Express, payment plan
Established 1966

Liros Gallery occupies three floors of a historic townhouse in Old Town Alexandria. The directors buy and sell art of the 16th through mid-20th century, with a special interest in old European and American paintings, as well as fine prints and an occasional drawing. Some of the artists whose works come up for sale have been: Edgar Hewitt Nye, Alfred Hockings, James Pollard, Piranesi, Kuniyoshi, Currier & Ives, and American primitive painters. Another area of great interest to George Liros and Karen Wesley are Russian and Greek icons. All pieces are guaranteed authentic.

Appraisals; restoration of paintings, prints, and frames; and custom framing services are available.

Finally, at their second location known as the Print Room, 320 King Street, Alexandria, 549-7883, selections include fine art reproductions, posters, and restrike engravings. Maps, prints, and engravings both old and new are also available there.

ANGEL NUÑEZ GALLERY

1516 Connecticut Avenue, N.W.
Washington, DC 20036
(202)328-7893
Monday-Saturday 10-8, Sunday 12-6

Owner/Director: Angel Nuñez
Price Range: $40-50,000
Cash, check, American Express,
payment plan
Established 1976

The ceilings of the Angel Nuñez Gallery are lined with huge crystal chandeliers, creating an eerie and elegant feeling all at the same time. *Objets* including African masks and oriental porcelains are available. In addition, the walls are lined with paintings by artists around the world. Most of the work is semi-antique.

THE OLD PRINT GALLERY

1220 31st Street, N.W.
Washington, DC 20007
(202)965-1818
Monday-Saturday 10-5:30
Member American Appraisers Association

Owners: James and Judith Blakely, James von Ruster
Cash, check, MasterCard, Visa
Established 1971

The Old Print Gallery has a large selection of original 18th and 19th century American prints and maps, as well as an occasional architectural piece or watercolor. Engravings by Winslow Homer and historic cartoonist Nast, as well as prints by George Catlin and Carl Bodmer, can be found alongside pieces by William Sidney Mount, Frederic Remington, and Audubon. Many natural history prints by European artists are available too.

OSUNA GALLERY

Even though Osuna is also known for his occasional Old Master shows, please see the Contemporary Galleries section.

PENSLER GALLERIES

2029 Q Street, N.W.
Washington, DC 20009
(202)328-9190
By appointment only

Owner/Director: Alan Pensler
Cash, check
Established 1979

Interested in paintings of all periods, Alan Pensler's special area of interest is in 19th century American paintings and drawings. Naive, folk, and early western art is available along with traditional European-influenced styles.

Pensler plans to re-open his gallery in 1988. In the meantime, he is doing business as a private dealer. A small but select stock of artwork is available.

THE PRINT ROOM

Please refer to Liros Gallery earlier in this chapter.

ST. LUKE'S GALLERY

1715 Q Street, N.W.
Washington, DC 20009
(202)328-2424
Tuesday-Saturday 11-6

Owner/Directors: Nizar and Ellen Jawdat
Price Range: $50-10,000+
Cash, check, American Express, payment plan
Established 1986

Located two blocks from the Dupont Circle Metro stop, St. Luke's is housed within a spacious townhouse on Q Street.

With Bach in the background and fresh coffee on the burner, continental hospitality prevails here. Owners Nizar and Ellen Jawdat were featured 10 years ago in an article in *Parade* about Americans abroad. U.S. citizens, they still spend time in their country home in Italy. During their trips abroad they acquire art.

St. Luke's specializes in 17th to 19th century art. Paintings, drawings, original prints and an occasional sculpture by European and American masters and their students and followers can be found here. Many very reasonably-priced drawings and prints are always in stock.

SEIDNER GALLERY

1333 New Hampshire Avenue, N.W.
Washington, DC 20036
(202)775-8212
11-6 Monday-Saturday

Owner/Directors: Frank and Lee Seidner
Price Range: $50-65,000
Cash, check, American Express
Established 1986

Located near Dupont Circle, the Seidner Gallery specializes in western European furniture and art dating from the Renaissance through the 19th century.

Frank Seidner, a foreign service officer for 20 years, collected art before going into business as a dealer. African art, Asian art, and 18th century Italian tiles interest him most, but in general all antiquities catch his attention. The Seidner Gallery reflects his broad interest in antiquities: he handles traditional forms of art, furniture, and decorative objects, as well as architectural ornamentation of historic interest.

STUDIO ANTIQUES, INC.

628 N. Washington Street
Alexandria, VA 22314
(703)548-5188
Monday-Saturday 10-5, Sunday 12-5

Owner/Directors: Richard Totoiu
and Lois Boyles
Price Range: $225 up
Cash, check, MasterCard, Visa
Established 1982

Studio Antiques, in a historic row house in Old Town, seems more like a rich uncle's overfurnished town home than the place of business for an antique and art dealer. Although the antiques which furnish the rooms are for sale, they seem more like props which complement the artwork, bringing it into an appropriate context.

Very fine paintings hang on every wall. The inventory is large. Prices are reasonable considering the quality of the work.

Studio Antiques handles 18th and 19th century European and American paintings in classical, realist styles. Occasionally deaccessions from the National Museum of American Art and other notable institutions are available.

TAGGART, JORGENSEN & PUTMAN GALLERY

3241 P Street, N.W.
Washington, DC 20007
(202)298-7676
Monday-Friday 10:30-5 and
  11-5 Saturday
Member Washington Art Dealers Association

Director: Lauren Plescia
Cash, check, payment plan
Established 1983

    The Taggart, Jorgensen & Putman Gallery specializes in 19th and early 20th century American oil and watercolor paintings, pastels, and drawings. Their sub-specialty is British watercolors of the last 100 years.
    The gallery is available for appraisal services, and staff is glad to offer advice on framing or restoration. They have assisted in building many fine private collections in the Washington area.
    Works by artists including the following have appeared at Taggart, Jorgensen & Putman: John Singer Sargent, Winslow Homer, Frank W. Benson, Childe Hassam, Edward W. Redfield, Martin Johnson Heade, Ernest Lawson, Jasper Cropsey, Sanford Gifford, William Harnett, Alfred Bricher, and others.

VEERHOFF GALLERIES

Please see the Contemporary Galleries section; although Veerhoff handles some historic art, most of it is by living American artists.

Art of Other Cultures, All Time Periods

AFFRICA

2010 1/2 R Street, N.W.
Washington, DC 20009
(202)745-7272
12-6 Wednesday through Saturday
 and by appointment
Member Washington Art Dealers Association
and DuPont Circle Fine Art Galleries

Owner/Director: Mona Gavigan
Price Range: $100 up
Cash, check, payment plan
Established 1979

Affrica, formerly known as Volta Place, handles traditional African art, featuring authentic objects made and used in both ritual and secular contexts.

The emphasis is on African objects of museum quality—in fact, museums are sometimes clients here. Sculpture, masks, textiles, weapons, implements, furniture, jewelry, and decorative objects of aesthetic and ethnographic merit are available. Most of the work is semi-antique to antique.

However, the art here is not necessarily expensive; beginning collectors are accommodated too with quality art objects at a good price.

Mona Gavigan is happy to share the background and lore of the work she deals in, all of which has genuinely been used within traditional African cultures. As a rule, the pieces were created by gifted artisans—people who created objects because they were truly artists, not because a relatively detached mode of making souvenir items would simply bring in trade goods. Much of the artwork available at this gallery was taken from Africa during the days when Europe was colonizing the continent.

GALLERIE LA TAJ

1203 King Street
Alexandria, VA 22314
(703)549-0508
12-5 Tuesday through Sunday
 and by appointment

Owner/Director: Theodore Toatley
Cash, check, MasterCard, Visa,
American Express, payment plan
Established 1983

A storefront gallery in Old Town, Gallerie La Taj handles traditionally executed, but contemporary, African as well as African-influenced art and craft work. One of the artists recently featured was Alexis Joyner, a black artist from southern Virginia.

HARMATTAN

216 7th Street, S.E.
Washington, DC 20003
(202)544-8444
Wednesday-Saturday 11-6, Sunday 12-5

Owner/Director: Cheryl Olkes
Cash, check, MasterCard, Visa,
American Express, payment plan
Established 1987

Harmattan deals in traditional west African and Morrocan textiles, sculpture, basketwork, and calabashes. Most pieces are contemporary, some are semi-antique.

HENDRICKS ART COLLECTION, LTD.

3841 Farragut Avenue
Kensington, MD 20895
(301)946-6334
By appointment
Member American Society of Appraisers

Owner/Director: Kappy Hendricks
Cash, check, MasterCard, Visa,
American Express, payment plan
Established 1965

Hendricks specializes in a "historical approach to Japanese woodblock prints," as well as Japanese etchings and silkscreens, c. 1800 to the present. Artists represented include Tadashi Nakayama, Kiyoshi Saito, Ryohei Tanaka, K. Sugiura, Yoshitoshi Mori, Clifton Karhu.

OLD WARSAW GALLERIES

Please see the Contemporary Galleries section.

SANDER FINE ART

2013 Q Street, N.W.
Washington, DC 20009
(202)265-4249
Tuesday-Friday 4:30-7, Saturday 2-5
Sunday 2-6, and by appointment

Owner/Director: Christine Sander
Cash, check
Established 1987

Christine Sander, from a family of art dealers, is handling some interesting contemporary art in her new English basement gallery space near Dupont Circle. She shows primarily far Eastern artists; one of her opening shows featured a show of dissident Chinese artists. Media include sculpture, paintings, and works on paper in contemporary styles. Sander discovers represented artists on her trips abroad.

SCHWEITZER JAPANESE PRINTS INC.

4309 Van Ness Street, N.W.
Washington, DC 20016
(202)363-0308
By appointment

Owner/Director: Paul R. Schweitzer
Price Range: $10.00-15,000
Cash, check, payment plan
Established 1968

Schweitzer is a private dealer of Japanese prints and paintings. Open "by appointment only anytime," work by about 100 Japanese artists, emerging to posthumous, is on hand—watermedia, drawings, prints; Hanga (contemporary Japanese graphics) and traditional Ukiyo-E.

Contemporary Japanese artists interested in representation may phone for an appointment.

SHOGUN GALLERY

1083 Wisconsin Avenue, N.W.
Second floor
Washington, DC 20007
(202)965-5454
Monday-Sunday 11-6

Owners: Toni Liberthson, Larry Everitt
Director: Gary Gestson
Price Range: $10.00 up
Cash, check, MasterCard, Visa, payment plan
Established 1978

Shogun Gallery deals in 18th through 20th century original Japanese woodblock prints, many of museum quality. Shogun handles the work of over 50 Japanese artists, including examples by famous masters like Hiroshige and Kuniyoshi as well as works by contemporary Japanese artists. Work by Utamaro, Yoshitoshi, Toyokuni III, and Hiroshi Yoshida is on hand.

TRIBES

2407 18th Street, N.W.
Washington, DC 20009
(202)387-1472
Thursday-Sunday noon-10
Affiliated with Tribes of Brussels and London

Owner/Director: Donald Peyton
Price Range: $50-5,000
Cash, check, payment plan
Established 1986

This unusual gallery handles fine semi-antique art and objects from over 20 African tribes, as well as Moroccan rugs and contemporary African sculpture. Protest works by Arthur Heleza, S. Williamson, Tony Maize, and others can be found here. Poetry readings, performances of African music, and discussions are sponsored as well.

The gallery is on the second floor above Nomad, an interesting store featuring clothes and accessories from around the world.

Contemporary American artists working in areas "relevant to African or Third World concerns" may phone for an appointment, or send a letter with slides and artist's statement.

TROCADÉRO

1501 Connecticut Avenue, N.W.
Washington, DC 20036
(202)234-5656
Tuesday-Saturday 10:30-6

Owner/Director: Kitty Higgins
Average Price Range: $500-5,000
Cash, check, MasterCard, Visa,
American Express, payment plan
Established 1978

Trocadéro, a.k.a. Kitty Higgins Far Eastern Art, handles a wide variety of Far Eastern art primarily from China and the Himalayas. Chinese ceramics, stone and bronze sculptures, religious objects, and paintings are usually available here. Some of the pieces date to before the birth of Christ.

TROCADÉRO TEXTILE ART

1501 Connecticut Avenue, N.W.
Washington, DC 20036
(202)328-8440
Tuesday-Saturday 10:30-6:30

Owner/Directors: Bill and Jane Seward
Price Range: $35.00-20,000
Cash, check, MasterCard, Visa,
American Express, payment plan
Established 1979

Although the two Trocadéros occupy the same building, they are separate enterprises. Trocadéro Textile Art handles textiles, including tapestries and rugs, from the Middle East. Some North and South American Indian works (Navajo, Andean) are available as well. Most pieces are antique and semi-antique, steeped in tradition; Bill Seward says, "Nomadic and village weavings are like folk music, the patterns are handed down from memory through the generations from mother to daughter."

ZYGOS GALLERY

Please see the Contemporary Galleries section for more information on Zygos Gallery.

MUSEUMS

ANACOSTIA NEIGHBORHOOD MUSEUM

1901 Fort Place, S.E.
Washington, DC 20020
(202)287-3369

Monday-Sunday 10-5
Admission free

One aim of Anacostia Neighborhood Museum is to contribute to the lives of residents of the rather depressed Anacostia area through exhibitions and resources. The primary aim, though, is to provide an important and accessible forum for the examination of the continuing issues of black Americans, including African themes and the social realities of being black in America today.

Changing exhibits are offered along with a regular program of lectures by distinguished black American artists. Sometimes art workshops are offered free of charge.

BARNEY STUDIO HOUSE

2306 Massachusetts Avenue, N.W.
Washington, DC 20008
(202)357-3111

By appointment only
Admission free

Alice Pike Barney, an heiress, was an artist whose resumé included the Paris Salon and studies with James McNeill Whistler and other notables. She was a one-person cultural arts center; besides painting every day, she was a whirlwind hostess who gave frequent soirées, salons, and socials in her home. Also a playwright, she helped to found the Sylvan Theater.

The house is full of paintings by Barney and her colleagues. Also worthy of note are the light fixtures designed by Tiffany.

Niagara Falls, 1857, by Frederic Edwin Church. Oil on canvas, 42^1/$_4$"x90^1/$_2$". Courtesy Corcoran Gallery of Art.

CORCORAN GALLERY OF ART

New York Avenue and 17th Street, N.W.
Washington, DC 20006
(202)638-3211

Tuesday-Sunday 10-4:30,
Thursday 10-9
Admission free unless blockbuster, but contribution requested

Established in 1859 and opened to the public in 1869, the Corcoran is Washington's oldest art museum and is one of the three oldest in the country. (The Metropolitan in New York and Boston Museum of Fine Arts are the other two.) The Corcoran originally operated in the building now housing the Renwick Gallery. The Corcoran opened in its current location in 1897.

The facade features a frieze bearing the name of 11 artists considered Great Masters in the 1890's. The name of only one American, Washington Allston, is there; this is ironic because the Corcoran has become best-known for its collection of American art as well as for its continuing support of relatively contemporary art.

The rotating exhibits have often proved to be "blockbusters." For example, while the National Gallery of Art was hosting Andrew Wyeth's "Helga" series, the Corcoran installed a show featuring the three generations of Wyeth painters.

Founder William Wilson Corcoran was photographed by Matthew Brady in the 1850's when the field of photography was in its infancy. The Corcoran has continued a tradition of supporting photography. The Corcoran is also sporadically supportive of Washington artists.

William Corcoran intended that aspiring artists be allowed to copy masterworks of the collection, and soon after the foundation of the Gallery a master teacher was hired. Soon several more teachers were needed and the Corcoran School of Art became an associated institution. It is still the only specialized school of art in Washington.

Berlin Abstraction, 1914-15, by Marsden Hartley. Oil on canvas, 32"x26". Courtesy Corcoran Gallery of Art.

DUMBARTON OAKS

1703 32nd Street, N.W.
Washington, DC 20007
(202)338-8278

Tuesday-Sunday 2-5
Admission free but contribution requested

A diplomat and his wife, Mr. and Mrs. Robert Woods Bliss, were the last private owners of Dumbarton Oaks. In 1940 they donated the estate and collection to Harvard University, but the diplomatic tradition at Dumbarton Oaks continued when in 1944 two international conferences were held there leading to the establishment of the United Nations.

The Blisses were scholarly collectors of pre-Columbian and Byzantine art. It is probably impossible to assemble a collection comprehensively surveying Western Hemisphere art of all cultures and times before the arrival of Columbus. Knowing this, Mr. Bliss simply continued to acquire the finest examples he could of native American art. He was partially responsible for the change in attitude toward artifacts. When he started collecting them, although such objects could be found in museums of natural history and anthropology, they were not yet considered art.

In 1963, a new wing designed by Philip Johnson was opened. It consists of eight glass cylinders arranged around a garden courtyard; each structure presents objects arranged by culture and chronology. The feeling is that the viewer is discovering these pieces in the native tropical settings of South America or Mexico.

The Byzantine collection includes some fine examples of pieces dating from 300 A.D. to the 1400's. Both religious and secular masterpieces are represented.

Dumbarton Oaks, which can be rented for private functions, is graced by 16 acres of lawns, formal gardens, pools, and fountains.

EVANS-TIBBS COLLECTION

1910 Vermont Avenue, N.W.
Washington, DC 20001
(202)234-8164

Wednesday-Thursday 6-8,
Saturday 2-5, and by appointment
Admission free

The Evans-Tibbs Collection, though officially on the books as a museum, is an unusual establishment because it is one of two museums in town where work is sometimes for sale. Fondo Del Sol is the other.

Once you find it—it is between T and U Streets, N.W., off 10th—you will see a permanent archival collection of Afro-American art, with changing shows featuring both historically important and contemporary black artists.

The house itself has an interesting history. It was designated a historic landmark in 1985, partly because it has enjoyed for nearly 100 years a reputation for being the meeting place for well-known blacks: Langston Hughes, Booker T. Washington, Bill "Bojangles" Robinson, and many others.

FONDO DEL SOL VISUAL ART AND MEDIA CENTER

2112 R Street, N.W.
Washington, DC 20008
(202)483-2777

Tuesday-Saturday 12:30-5:30
Admission: Contributions accepted

Fondo del Sol, which means "center of the sun," is dedicated to the arts of all the Americas. It is the oldest artist-run museum in the United States.

Fondo del Sol was founded in 1973 by a group of South, Central, and North American artists and writers. For four years, they worked primarily in schools with Latino youth. Then in 1977 the Center was opened in its present location, a townhouse near Dupont Circle, with grants from the National Endowment for the Arts and other foundations and individuals.

The founders had established some powerful connections; in 1977, in cooperation with the National Collection of Fine Arts (now the National Museum of American Art) they organized the first international touring exhibition of contemporary Latin-American artists. In 1983 Fondo del Sol joined with six other museums to found the Dupont-Kalorama Museum Consortium.

Fondo del Sol continues its program of support to individuals and groups of Latin-American and other American minority artists. Video art is an important medium here. The Media Center produces and/or assists filmmakers in producing films, and it distributes and exhibits films, videos, and TV documentaries about ethnic groups.

Besides offering exhibit space to contemporary artists, it features performance art programs as well as lectures, readings and concerts. A highlight is the annual music festival of salsa and reggae.

Nandi. India, 13th-14th century. Bronze.
Courtesy Freer Gallery of Art.

FREER GALLERY OF ART

Jefferson Drive and 12th Street, S.W.
Washington, DC 20560
(202)357-2104

Sunday-Saturday 10-5:30
Admission free

In 1904, the bachelor industrialist Charles Freer made arrangements that his personal collection would be accepted by the Smithsonian upon his death, on the condition that the federal government would maintain the collection, neither loaning nor deaccessioning any pieces. He included in his bequest more than a million dollars for the construction of a building on the Mall to house the collection.

When Freer died in 1919, his collection consisted of almost 9,000 pieces of Oriental art and over 1,250 works by James McNeill Whistler, a close friend who influenced Freer strongly.

The collection consists of over 25,000 pieces now. Besides the Whistler collection, the Freer is a museum of Asian and near Eastern art from the third millenium B.C. to the early 20th century. Rotating exhibits drawing from the permanent collection feature only a fraction of it: Chinese bronzes; Islamic paintings and calligraphy; Japanese screens; Chinese porcelains; Buddhist and Hindu sculpture; Greek, Aramaic, and Armenian biblical manuscripts; early Christian paintings; and other art treasures from the Near and Far East.

A feature of the Freer is the Peacock Room created by Whistler in the 1870's. Originally a London dining room, it was unconventional and at times controversial, depending on who owned this architectural piece. After several owners lived in it, including an art dealer who displayed it as an "installation" in his London gallery, Freer purchased it in 1904.

The collection also contains more than 200 works by American artists who were Whistler's contemporaries.

Beaker, Syria, late 13th century. Glass, enameled and gilded.
Courtesy Freer Gallery of Art.

HILLWOOD

4155 Linnean Avenue, N.W.
Washington, DC 20008
(202)686-0410

Wednesday-Saturday and Monday 9-4:30
Admission $7; children under 12 not admitted

Marjorie Merriweather Post's third husband, Joseph E. Davies, was a diplomat assigned to the Soviet Union from 1936 to 1938, at a time when the Russians were liquidating church and imperial treasures. During those years Marjorie Post bought Russian paintings, porcelains, *objets d'art*, and other treasures literally by the pound.

Hillwood houses the only piece of Russian imperial regalia in existence outside the Soviet Union. An imperial nuptial crown made in 1840 was worn at the weddings of the last three czarinas; it is encrusted with 300 carats of diamonds. There are also 90 Fabergé objects including Imperial Easter eggs.

Other Russian treasures include gold and silver chalices, religious icons, *niello* boxes, floor-to-ceiling portraits of Russian czars and czarinas, and a Russian rock crystal chandelier.

HIRSHHORN MUSEUM AND SCULPTURE GARDEN

Independence Avenue and 8th Street, S.W.
Washington, DC 20560
(202)357-2700

Sunday-Saturday 10-5:30
Admission free

When emigré mining magnate Joseph Hirshhorn donated his collection to the Smithsonian in 1966, it became the first federal museum of contemporary art. By the time he died in 1981 the collection consisted of over 12,000 pieces.

The Hirshhorn is best known for its collection of late 19th century and early 20th century sculpture, featuring representative pieces by Rodin, Picasso, Moore, Rickey, di Suvero, Smith, Degas, Gauguin, Maillol, Matisse, Daumier, Calder. Some of these can be leisurely contemplated in the accessible sculpture garden; many more are inside.

Hirshhorn was sympathetic to fellow immigrants who had fled Europe. He was one of the first to collect the Abstract Expressionists. He collected new work by new artists of all persuasions whether they were known or not; it has been said that he made many an artist, because when he discovered someone whose work he respected, he often bought many pieces and would stimulate others to collect too.

The Hirshhorn offers surveys, some more completely rounded out than others, of major trends in late 19th and 20th century European and American art. The permanent collection is a world-class accumulation of recent Western art.

Changing exhibitions also offer retrospectives of currently active professional "star" artists and an occasional group show by same.

LIBRARY OF CONGRESS

10 1st Street, S.E.
Washington, DC 20540
(202)287-5000

Monday-Friday 8:30 a.m.-9:30 p.m., Saturday 8:30-6
Reading rooms 9-5:30 Monday-Saturday
Admission free

As perhaps the most complete library in the world, the Library of Congress serves as a repository of printed matter. Thus it also holds one of the greatest collections of prints and photographs in the world.

The beauty of the building itself is complemented by "Early Public Art" in the form of murals, sculpture, and hand-made architectural details. Almost 100 American artists participated in the making of art about knowledge and learning for this building.

MUSEUM OF MODERN ART OF LATIN AMERICA

201 18th Street, N.W.
Washington, DC 20006
(202)458-6016, -6019

Tuesday-Saturday 10-5
Admission free

The Museum of Modern Art of Latin America exhibits mainly contemporary work by Latin American artists. In 1957, Ambassador Luis Quintanilla, the Mexican representative to the Organization of American States (OAS), proposed that the organization purchase one work from each OAS show to build a collection of Latin American art. Donations started coming in as well and the collection quickly grew. The permanent collection now holds over 900 works produced during the last 40 years, including work by Matta, Tamayo, Botero, and other great artists. Naive works by Haitian and other artists are also in the collection.

Changing exhibits feature the new work of currently practicing artists.

The museum also administers an adjunct gallery in the OAS building at Constitution Avenue and 17th Street, N.W. The sculpture garden is a highlight.

NATIONAL AIR AND SPACE MUSEUM

Independence Avenue and 6th Street, S.W.
Washington, DC 20560
(202)357-2700

Sunday-Saturday 10-5:30
Admission free, but some special exhibits,
i.e. movies, have admission charges

The wonderful attractions here go beyond fantastic and comprehensive surveys of the history and adventure of flight, and films which are masterpieces.

Sculptures by Charles O. Perry, Richard Lippold, and Alejandro Otero command attention outside. Art installations inside include murals by Keith Ferris and Eric Sloane.

A program called "Flight and the Arts" offers changing exhibitions of paintings, drawings, sculpture, prints, and photographs by contemporary artists showing aviation art and other artistic perceptions of air and space.

NATIONAL GALLERY OF ART

Constitution Avenue and 6th Street, N.W.
Washington, DC 20565
(202)737-4215

Monday-Saturday 10-5,
Sunday 10-9
Admission free

The National Gallery of Art surveys Western art from the late medieval period through Post-Impressionism and includes some art representative of 20th century movements (No permanent place in the Gallery is accorded to an artist unless s/he has been dead for 20 or more years). The majority of works are paintings.

Millionaire industrialist and treasury secretary Andrew Mellon was personally financially responsible for the Gallery's opening in 1941. The Mellon family was responsible for the construction of National Gallery's East Wing, too. The Mellon collection still comprises a large portion of its foundation. Operated federally, the Gallery continues to rely on private donations to fulfill its acquisitions; it has been said that the National Gallery is actually a collection of collections. Other great collectors have contributed: the Kress brothers gave their vast collection of Italian masterpieces, the Wideners of Philadelphia were best known for their contribution of decorative arts and Chinese porcelains, Lessing J. Rosenwald's collection of prints and drawings established the National Gallery as an important graphics collection, and financier Chester Dale contributed his 19th and 20th century French paintings.

The National Gallery has one of the finest collections of Flemish and Dutch paintings in the world, and possesses the largest number of Vermeers in one museum outside of Holland. The French Impressionist collection is magnificent.

The National Gallery of Art is famous for its "blockbuster" exhibitions such as King Tut, the Luminists, Andrew Wyeth. The National Gallery is visited by more people than any other art museum in the world.

NATIONAL GALLERY OF ART, EAST WING

Constitution Avenue and 4th Street, N.W.
Washington, DC 20565
(202)737-4215

Monday-Saturday 10-5,
Sunday 12-9
Admission free

The intention of the National Gallery of Art is to cover the entire history of Western art. The East Wing, on the other hand, is devoted entirely to 20th century art. The building itself is a work of art by architect I. M. Pei.

With natural light pouring in through skylights, and with enough vertical and horizontal space to make a soaring bird happy, the central atrium houses several large-scale 20th century masterpieces which were commissioned specifically for this building. A Calder mobile drifts ponderously yet cheerfully upon natural air currents; a Miro tapestry "Woman" challenges all who approach; a Motherwell painting, "Reconciliation Elegy," is fated ever to move in upon itself without moving.

The permanent collection features in-depth surveys of the work of Ellsworth Kelly, Mark Rothko, Robert Rauschenberg, and Sam Francis. A gallery beautifully lit by skylights features the sculptures of David Smith. Gorky, Picasso, Matisse, Kline, and other already historical figures are also well-represented.

To complement the permanent collection, exhibitions concentrating on some facet of relatively new art are regularly curated and installed.

An underground corridor connects the East Wing to the rest of the National Gallery.

Femme, 1977, by Jean Miro. Tapestry, approx. 33'x19'. Courtesy National Gallery of Art, East Wing.

Mask (pwo), Chokwe peoples, Zaire and Angola. Wood, fiber, metal. Photograph by Jeffrey Plosonka. Courtesy National Museum of African Art.

NATIONAL MUSEUM OF AFRICAN ART

950 Independence Avenue, S.W.
Washington, DC 20560
(202)357-4600

Monday-Sunday 10-5:30
Admission free

The National Museum of African Art has moved from Capitol Hill to a spacious, beautiful underground site next to the Arthur M. Sackler Gallery. It is accessed by a six-domed entrance pavilion in the Enid A. Haupt Garden, in the quadrangle bounded by Independence Avenue, the Smithsonian Castle, the Freer Gallery, and the Arts and Industries building. The National Museum of African Art is one of only two museums in the nation devoted to the collection and exhibition of African art. The museum works primarily with art from south of the Sahara, since northern African art generally falls into the Middle Eastern category of scholarship.

The National Museum of African Art was founded in 1964 by Warren Robbins, a former diplomat. Robbins, a collector, was at first interested in African art as it influenced modern art, but he soon realized that African art was a complete, fascinating field in and of itself. Initially a private educational institution, the Museum of African Art became part of the Smithsonian complex in 1979.

More than 6,000 objects of functional, decorative, secular, religious, ornamental, and ritual use comprise the collection of carved wooden and mixed media masks and fertility figures, textiles, and brass pieces dating from the 13th century. Some of the museum's exhibitions explore broad themes in African art; others are devoted to the arts of a single ethnic or geographic group.

An unusual feature of the museum is the Eliot Elisofon Photographic Archive, named after the *Life* photographer. The archive consists of a permanent collection of 150,000 color slides, 70,000 black-and-white photographs, feature films, and over 120,000 feet of unedited film footage on African art and culture.

Divination cup, Yoruba peoples, Nigeria. Wood. Photograph by Bruce Fleischer. Courtesy National Museum of African Art.

People in the Sun, 1960, by Edward Hopper. Oil on canvas, $40^{3}/8" \times 60^{3}/8"$. Courtesy National Museum of American Art.

NATIONAL MUSEUM OF AMERICAN ART

8th and G Streets, N.W.
Washington, DC 20560
(202)357-3176

Monday-Sunday 10-5:30
Admission free

Formerly known as the National Collection of Fine Arts, the National Museum of American Art (NMAA) is the oldest U.S. federal art collection; its beginnings pre-date the founding of the Smithsonian Institution. However, it was absorbed by the Smithsonian in 1860.

NMAA's focus is to collect American art from the colonial era to the present. It has acquired masterpieces from the Hudson River, American Impressionist, and many other American schools and genres; NMAA currently has the largest collection of 1930's art produced under the federal art programs. The museum is laid out chronologically, the earliest work being on the first floor and 20th century art on the third floor.

The building housing NMAA has seen many uses. During the Civil War, the building served as barracks, hospital and morgue. Lincoln's second inaugural ball was held there. The Patent Office occupied the building, then the Civil Service Commission. In 1957 a hotly contested bill was introduced in Congress to raze the building and construct a parking garage. Art won.

The National Museum of American Art is host to frequent special events, including retrospectives and lectures by famous artists, concerts, and children's workshops. By appointment, the conservation department provides consultation on the care and handling of works of art.

A large fountained courtyard connects NMAA to the National Portrait Gallery which fronts F Street.

Part of the museum's collection spawned an adjunct museum, the Renwick Gallery, which opened in 1972 to house and display American design, crafts, and decorative arts. The Barney Studio House is administered by NMAA as well.

Buffalo Bull's Back Fat, Head Chief, Blood Tribe, 1832, by George Catlin. Oil on canvas, 29"x24". Courtesy National Museum of American Art.

NATIONAL MUSEUM OF AMERICAN HISTORY

Constitution Avenue and 14th Street, N.W.
Washington, DC 20560
(202)357-2700

Monday-Sunday 10-5:30
Admission free

Infinity, a stainless steel sculpture (1967) by José de Riviera, was the first piece of abstract art ever commissioned by the federal government. It guards the Mall entrance of the National Museum of American History. *The Gwenfritz*, a 40-foot tall, 35-ton black steel sculpture by Alexander Calder, stands on the grounds too near 14th Street and Constitution Avenue.

On the third floor's West Wing is a large collections of ceramics, porcelains, and glass, some dating from 100 B.C.

NATIONAL MUSEUM OF WOMEN IN THE ARTS

1250 New York Avenue, N.W.
Washington, DC 20005
(202)783-5000

Tuesday-Saturday 10-5,
Sunday 12-5
Admission free

The National Museum of Women in the Arts opened in 1987 amidst controversy and discomfort. While some objected to the "ghettoization" of women artists, others rejoiced that women have been allowed entrance into a formal museum, even if it is a new one.

Wilhelmina ("Billie") Holladay and her husband, Wallace Holladay, have been avid collectors of art by women for many years. They were attracted to the specialty of women artists because they felt that women artists had never been taken seriously. Even worse than "ghettoization" to them was their impression that works by women were being downright ignored. Learning that less than five percent of the work in national museums had been done by women, they resolved to study this field. They were shocked to find that there *was* no field—no scholarly work had been done in this area before. Even H. W. Janson's book *History of Art*, the standard art history tome, acknowledged not a single woman artist in its 500-plus pages until the 1980's when reader demand and cultural pressure finally resulted in mention of one woman artist, Mary Cassatt.

Somehow poignant in the context of the shrouded nature of the field of women artists, this private museum is housed in a building with a past. It was once one of many porno movie meccas on its street. It has also housed a temple for a local lodge of the Masonic organization, which—like the field of women artists—has been secret. But the Renaissance Revival building designed by Waddy Wood was renovated, and the phoenix rose from the rubble. It is now a museum of architectural grandeur.

Changing exhibits are curated around themes like "American Women Artists, 1830-1930," its opening exhibit. Also on the schedule are exhibits of contemporary works from each of the 50 states. In the interests of equality, the exhibits not specifically exploring women's themes will include the work of men too.

Flowers in a Vase, by Rachel Ruysch (1664-1750). Oil on canvas, $18^{3}/4" \times 15^{3}/4"$.
Courtesy National Museum of Women in the Arts.

NATIONAL PORTRAIT GALLERY

8th and F Streets, N.W.
Washington, DC 20560
(202)357-2700

Monday-Sunday 10-5:30
Admission free

The National Portrait Gallery specializes in portrait works of Americans.

The word "portrait" can conjure up somber visions of medium-sized oil paintings of businessmen seated in their boardrooms or perched upon their desks, darkly lit. But the National Portrait Gallery has been blessed with imaginative donors and curators.

Man Ray's photograph of Ernest Hemingway, and James Montgomery Flagg's large painting of the 1919 Dempsey-Willard fight are certainly not formal boardroom portraits.

The Hall of Presidents presents haunting, insightful images of people whom cameras were invented too late for. And presidential portraits executed after the advent of photography offer insights into sometimes more informal sides.

Another notable feature of the Gallery is its collection of *Time* magazine portrait covers. Although Jimmy Carter was known for being the first frequent presidential blue-jeans wearer, Reagan is the one clad in jeans and a western shirt in the National Portrait Gallery.

Special events include "Portraits in Motion" dramatizations by some of the great living American storytellers. Jon Spelman is a regular.

By prior arrangement, portraits may be brought in on Thursdays for the curators or conservators to examine and advise.

Last but not least, the National Portrait Gallery has on file resumés and photographs of works by contemporary living portrait artists.

THE PHILLIPS COLLECTION

1600-1612 21st Street, N.W.
Washington, DC 20009
(202)387-0961

Tuesday-Saturday 10-5, Sunday 2-7
Admission: Contribution requested

Based on a family collection of then-modern art, the Phillips gallery opened in 1921 in Duncan Phillip's home. The Phillips Collection is now world-famous for its 19th and 20th century French paintings and for its collection of American modernist works; important collections of the works of American masters such as John Marin and Georgia O'Keeffe as well as major paintings by the French Impressionists form the backbone of the collection.

The Phillips is undergoing extensive renovations to expand and improve the space which will be devoted to changing exhibitions; completion is scheduled for early 1989. In the meantime, the museum performs admirably, putting on special exhibitions featuring recent and contemporary masters, and special lectures.

A museum tradition is the Sunday Afternoon Concert Series. Concerts are performed Sunday evenings at 5 p.m., September through May, unless it is on Easter or Christmas. Admission is free, seating unreserved.

Two Sculptors, by Honoré Daumier (1808-79). Oil on wood panel, $10^1/2$"x14". Courtesy The Phillips Collection.

Shore Front, 1938, by Arthur Dove. Wax emulsion on canvas, 22"x36". Courtesy The Phillips Collection.

Desert Landscape, 1980, by Frank Fleming. Hand-built porcelain, unglazed, 14 1/2"x30"x21". Courtesy Renwick Gallery, National Museum of American Art.

RENWICK GALLERY

Pennsylvania Avenue and 17th Street, N.W.
Washington, DC 20560
(202)357-2700

Monday-Sunday 10-5:30
Admission free

The Renwick, a curatorial department of the National Museum of American Art, presents special exhibitions of historic and contemporary American craft, design, and decorative art. Exhibitions featuring such art from other nations are also regularly presented to complement the U.S. program.

The Renwick was named after the architect, James Renwick, Jr., who designed the building. "The extraordinary atmosphere of the building itself makes the museum's principal point: design is not an isolated element but affects all that we do," said Joshua Taylor in 1972. At the time he was director of the National Collection of Fine Arts, now known as the National Museum of American Art.

The Renwick Gallery opened in 1972 after extensive renovation; it is one of Washington's newest art museums. But the building itself formerly housed the Corcoran, one of the oldest museum collections in the country.

The Renwick's museum shop is an unusual one; it frequently carries some of the best craft work available by living American artists who have been selected by a nationwide jury process.

Frequent lectures and demonstrations by noted craft artists are scheduled, along with concerts and films.

Music Stand, 1975, by Wendell Castle. Walnut, 42"x26"x19". Courtesy Renwick Gallery, National Museum of American Art.

Carved box, China, Ming dynasty (1368-1644). Lacquer on wood, ivory inlay. Courtesy Arthur M. Sackler Gallery.

ARTHUR M. SACKLER GALLERY

1050 Independence Avenue, S.W.
Washington, DC 20560
(202)357-2700

Monday-Sunday 10-5:30
Admission free

The Sackler Gallery and the National Museum of African Art are the Smithsonian's newest additions. Arthur M. Sackler, a medical researcher, publisher, and art collector, pledged over 1,000 Asian masterworks to the Smithsonian, as well as $4 million toward construction of a museum to house the treasures. Sackler's gift was intended to complement the Freer collection and to concentrate on styles and types of Asian and near Eastern art not generally accessible. For example, the Sackler collection includes a number of 20th century Chinese paintings, an area of scholarship which has only recently opened up.

Located underground, the Sackler Gallery is accessed by an entrance pavilion in the Enid A. Haupt Garden, in the quadrangle bounded by Independence Avenue, the Smithsonian Castle, the Freer Gallery, and the Arts and Industries building.

It is strange to go underground to see the thousand-plus Asian masterpieces which were given to the Smithsonian by the late Arthur M. Sackler. It is like a fantasy of discovering the hushed interior of a pyramid. Everything is still; the interior is laid out respectfully and quietly. The interior architecture is fascinating—details such as latticework, columns, specially carved platforms and benches, niches, and gateways set off these Asian treasures beautifully. Expertly designed lighting adds to the feeling of splendor.

It is well worth a trip underground to see these ancient Chinese bronze vessels, Indian sculptures, jade carvings of exquisitely intricate detail, carved lacquer pieces of unbelievable sophistication, Chinese paintings, silver and gold pieces, and other objects.

Leaf from an album of 13 paintings, by Shitao (1642-1707), China, Qing dynasty. Ink and color on paper. Courtesy Arthur M. Sackler Gallery.

THE TEXTILE MUSEUM

2320 S Street, N.W.
Washington, DC 20008
(202)667-0441

Tuesday-Saturday 10-5, Sunday 1-5
Admission: Contribution requested

The Textile Museum is a privately operated, non-profit museum institution. Founded in 1925 by George Hewitt Myers, a collector, the museum today offers a survey of more than 10,000 textiles and 1,000 rugs. The collection consists of textiles primarily from Turkey, Iran, India, Indonesia, China, Egypt, and Spain. Pre-Columbian and Peruvian textiles, and smaller holdings from other regions of the world, round out the collection.

Changing exhibitions, publications, and educational programs encourage the appreciation of the beauty and significance of textiles as art; they also serve to illuminate the historical, cultural, and even familial context in which the textiles were made.

The museum is housed in two historic residences. The stately museum entrance, built in 1916, was originally the entrance to Myers' home. The architect was John Russell Pope, who was also the architect of the National Gallery of Art. Waddy B. Wood, who was the architect of the Woodrow Wilson house and the National Museum of Women in the Arts building, designed the other Textile Museum house in 1908.

A formal garden is open to the public.

OTHER SPACES EXHIBITING ART

Art Centers
College and University Art Galleries
Alternative Spaces

Art Centers

ARLINGTON ARTS CENTER

3550 Wilson Boulevard
Arlington, VA 22201
(703)524-1494, -1596
Tuesday-Saturday 11-5

Director: Katherine Freshley
Cash, check, payment plan
Established 1976

Going to the Arlington Arts Center can bring on *déjà vu* because it is like going back to primary school. The Center was formerly an Arlington County public school, the kind with the larger-than-life flight of concrete stairs leading up to the front door, the imposing entrance hall, hardwood floors, 12-foot ceilings, and big windows.

Arlington Arts Center has about 700 members in the metropolitan area. The building houses three galleries and several artists' studios. The Center's stated purpose is to show and support artists of demonstrated talent who live and work in Maryland, Virginia, and Washington, D.C. by providing monthly exhibit and educational programs as well as making studio space available. It hosts one-person and group shows, some of which are open area-wide juried competitions. A wide variety of styles and media are shown here.

Besides drawing and painting classes, as well as open life drawing sessions, a vital education program includes workshops and lectures by local gallery directors, critics, and other art professionals. A regular critique program also offers artists the chance to receive feedback from the same calibre of people.

THE ART BARN

2401 Tilden Street, N.W.
Washington, DC 20008
(202)426-6719
Wednesday-Saturday 10-5, Sunday 12-5

Director: Brian Smith
Cash, check, payment plan
Established 1971

Located in Rock Creek Park next to the Creek itself, the rustically beautiful two-story Art Barn was once the carriage house of the 150-year-old Peirce Plantation. Peirce Mill, with its working water wheel, is a few steps away.

Art Barn's purpose is to give Washington area professional artists—generally about 100 per year—a place to show. A group of five or more artists submits a proposal/application to the Exhibitions Committee for a group show. In conjunction with the exhibit, participating artists are encouraged to give a demonstration each weekend, for which they are paid, although such events are free to the public. Art Barn also hosts festivals, poetry readings, and other art events.

The National Park Service takes care of the building and grounds; the Art Barn Association, through membership and other fundraising, manages the exhibitions and the cultural and educational programs. Media and styles shown vary.

THE ART LEAGUE

105 North Union Street
Alexandria, VA 22314
(703)683-1780
Monday-Saturday 10-5

Director: Cora Rupp
Cash, check, MasterCard, Visa
Established 1974

Located in the Torpedo Factory Arts Center, the Art League is a thriving organization with nearly 800 members.

Their galleries on the first floor feature monthly membership exhibits juried by well-known regional gallery directors, art professors, artists, and other art professionals. Generally the work shown in the Art League galleries is representational work, usually in the many two-dimensional media.

The Art League's classrooms are on the upper floors, where courses in painting, drawing, printmaking, photography, architectural ("stained") glass, sculpture, ceramics, fiber arts, and other media are taught. The classes are led by some of the finest artists in the area, and tuitions, payable on a per-course basis, are reasonable.

The Art League also sponsors lectures and workshops by noted artists and arts professionals.

THE ATHENAEUM

201 Prince Street
Alexandria, VA 22314
(703)548-0035
Tuesday-Saturday 10-4

Director: Audrey Mitchell
Cash, check
Established 1961

The Athenaeum is a 19th century Greek revival historic property administered by the Northern Virginia Fine Arts Association. Inside—past the huge columns and entranceway—is a beautifully lit, high-ceilinged, two-room gallery.

A membership organization, it sponsors monthly exhibits featuring curated solo and group shows as well as open juried shows. The new contemporary work shown here is often highly abstract and sometimes experimental.

CAPITAL GALLERY

Please refer to Montpelier Cultural Arts Center in this chapter.

CIRCLE GALLERY

3232 P Street, N.W. (courtyard)
Washington, DC 20007
(202)333-2663
Tuesday-Saturday 11-4

Director: Joey Kossow
Cash, check
Established 1985

Circle Gallery is associated with the Washington Studio School, where classes in painting and drawing are offered.

Often, work shown at Circle is steeped in classical traditions, with an emphasis on representational styles. However, artists from "little-known to well-known, local to national" are given exposure here. The gallery directors are Washington Studio School faculty, and they have expressed interest in more abstract styles as well.

Monthly critiques and open life drawing sessions are sponsored as well.

GLEN ECHO GALLERY

Glen Echo Park
Glen Echo, MD 20812
(301)492-6229

Cash, check, MasterCard, Visa
Established 1975

As space becomes available, an area-wide juried competition is held for the right to rent the huts in Glen Echo Park as studio spaces. Competition is keen, and the quality of applicants is high. Changing exhibits at the Glen Echo Gallery feature the work of Glen Echo resident artists.

Resident artists also give classes; a wide variety of reasonably-priced courses are offered in many media. Glen Echo is administered by the National Park Service in cooperation with the Parks and History Association.

GREATER RESTON ARTS CENTER

11400 Washington Plaza West
Reston, VA 22090
(703)471-9242
Tuesday-Saturday 10-5, Sunday 12-5

Director: Anne Thomas
Cash, check, MasterCard, Visa, payment plan
Established 1968

Generally referred to as GRACE, the Greater Reston Arts Center offers regular exhibits and an educational program.

Changing exhibits feature work by GRACE members, community residents, and students. In addition, juried shows often are sponsored. One ambitious show, "A World Without Hunger," featured art by children throughout the world. Generally, though, the shows are area-wide competitions open to professional artists.

A wide variety of media and styles is always available at the gallery.

The educational program consists of varied classes, as well as an outreach program in which member artists take up residence in Reston area schools for a number of days.

GREEN SPRING GALLERY

4601 Green Spring Road
Alexandria, VA 22312
(703)941-6066
Sunday-Friday 12-4

Cash, check, MasterCard, Visa
Established 1970

The beautiful manor which houses the Fairfax County Council of the Arts (FCCA) and Green Spring Gallery was built in 1760. It is still surrounded by stately gardens and acreage.

The gallery, on the first floor, is operated "to promote local talent and encourage and strengthen [art] in Fairfax County." Regular exhibitions feature art by area students, professional artists, and arts organizations. FCCA, on the second floor, maintains a slide registry of Fairfax County artists.

FCCA also sponsors an annual Art in Public Places competition; artists from the metropolitan area are invited to submit slides. Accepted artists exhibit at Green Spring Gallery, as well as at several other government and corporate locations in the area.

MONTPELIER CULTURAL ARTS CENTER

12826 Laurel-Bowie Road
Laurel, MD 20708
(301)953-1993
Monday-Sunday 10-5

Director: Richard Zandler
Cash, check; some resident artists accept credit cards and/or set up payment plans
Established 1979

Montpelier Cultural Arts Center, in a lovely rural setting, is just off the Baltimore-Washington Parkway. It is a huge facility—over 4,300 sq. ft.—consisting of three galleries and several artists' studios. For whatever it's worth, it is the area's only gallery or art center which has an elevator.

Montpelier regularly sponsors area-wide juried exhibitions and other shows featuring local artists and arts organizations. In addition, through the Mid-Atlantic Arts Foundation, each year they are able to host a Resident Artist, usually a nationally known professional who has excelled in his/her field for some time.

An excellent educational program has been an important part of Montpelier's operations for many years. A full range of courses offers first-class instruction in a variety of media.

Also of interest, Montpelier administers the Capital Gallery, which is located within the well-trafficked Capital Centre. The gallery is open during Capital Centre events.

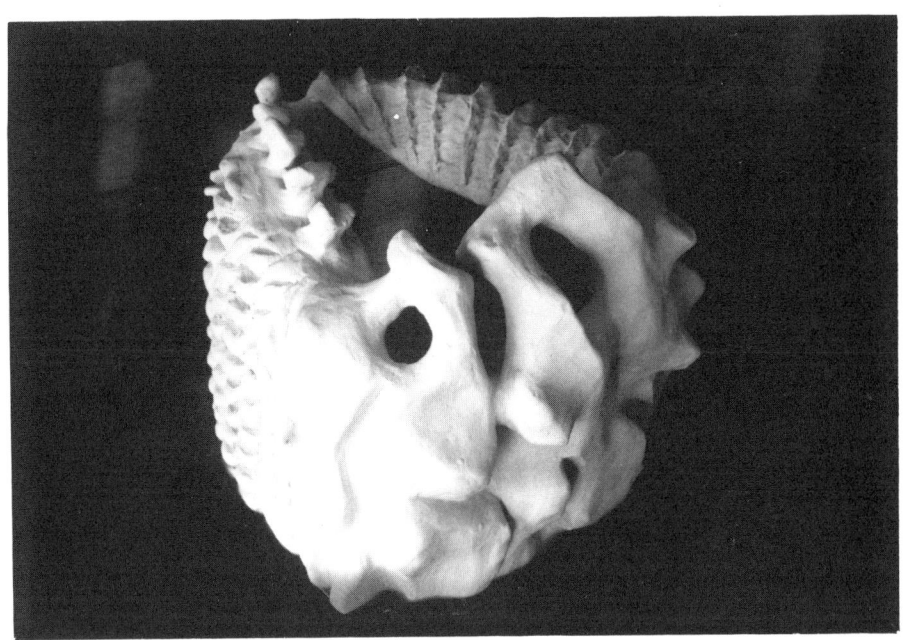

Universe III, 1986, by Genie Pearson. Ceramic, 20"x22"x32".
The New Art Center.

THE NEW ART CENTER

6925 Willow Street, N.W.
Washington, DC 20012
(202)291-2999
Wednesday-Sunday 11-5

Director: Jane Carpenter
Cash, check, payment plan
Established 1973

The New Art Center, formerly known as Washington Women's Art Center, moved into its new headquarters at the Takoma Metro Arts Center in 1986. Its gallery is on the ground floor at the end of a long, art-filled hallway.

The New Art Center sponsors several juried shows each year; noted arts professionals serve as jurors or, occasionally, curators. Women's themes still appear on the agenda, but so do many other social themes.

New Art Center serves as a checkpoint resource where artists may grow by participating in seminars, group critiques, and regular exhibitions. Artists may serve on curatorial and other committees.

Other arts events are also sponsored, such as poetry readings, salons, concerts, and lectures.

PAUL VI INSTITUTE FOR THE ARTS

924 G Street, N.W.
Washington, DC 20001
(202)347-1450
Hours vary, call first

Director: Dr. Tescia Ann Yonkers
Cash, check
Established 1977

Located near the Martin Luther King Library, Paul VI Institute for the Arts is a Catholic-sponsored organization. Dr. Tescia Yonkers is committed to exhibiting work of general spiritual significance by contemporary emerging American artists, regardless of race or creed. Local, previously unexhibited artists are especially encouraged to apply for an exhibition.

Paul VI regularly sponsors juried exhibitions with spiritual themes.

NORTHERN VIRGINIA FINE ARTS ASSOCIATION

Please see The Athenaeum, whose full name is Northern Virginia Fine Arts Association at the Athenaeum. They are profiled near the beginning of this chapter.

STRATHMORE HALL ARTS CENTER

10701 Rockville Pike
Bethesda, MD 20852
(301)530-0540
Monday-Friday 10-4, Saturday 10-3

Director: Eliot Pfanstiehl
Cash, check, MasterCard, Visa
Established 1983

In an elegant 10-room mansion built in 1915, Strathmore Hall Arts Center is a showcase for the visual, literary and performing arts. Special features include a gift shop, tea room, and sculpture garden.

Each year artists are invited to submit proposals for group or one-person shows. A variety of media and styles is shown. An annual juried exhibition is sponsored as well.

TORPEDO FACTORY ART CENTER
[See Color Plate after page 64]

105 North Union Street
Alexandria, VA 22314
(703)838-4565
Monday-Sunday 10-5

Methods of payment vary from studio to studio
Established 1974

The Torpedo Factory Art Center takes up an entire city block and houses over 200 professional artists and their studios, four cooperative galleries, and the Art League galleries and school. Most two- and three-dimensional media are practiced at Torpedo Factory: painting, drawing, printmaking, fiber arts, ceramics, sculpture (bronze, wood, marble, etc.), glass, jewelry, photography. So that visitors may see the artists at work, many of these studios are open to the public seven days a week.

A joint public/private venture, Torpedo Factory Art Center is a magnificent example of city redevelopment and adaptive re-use of public architecture. From 1918 through World War II, the building was a factory which manufactured—you guessed it—torpedoes. Then it was used as a storage facility by the Smithsonian and other branches of the Federal government. In 1974, the Art League and the Alexandria Bicentennial Commission co-proposed that the building be renovated for use as an art center. In May of that year artists began using fire hoses and bulldozers to remove 40 truckloads of debris, and in September it was being used as an artists' studio building.

Torpedo Factory Art Center is host to several small cooperative galleries: Enamelists, Potomac Craftsmen, Scope, and Factory Photoworks. In addition, 10 cooperative studios are in the building: five ceramics studios (Fire One, Going to Pot, Hollins Hills Potters, Studio 24, Waterfront Pottery); Fiber Gallery (wearables), Metalum (jewelry), and three studios producing prints (Discover Graphics, Mezzanine Multiples, and Printmakers Incorporated).

All artists who contract as studio tenants must first go through a jury process, possibly a waiting list, and agree to be open to the public at least 24 hours per week.

WASHINGTON PROJECT FOR THE ARTS (WPA)

434 7th Street, N.W.
Washington, DC 20004
(202)347-4813
Monday-Friday 10-6, Saturday 11-5

Director: Jock Reynolds
Sales referred to artist
Established 1975

The Washington Project for the Arts (WPA) is probably the most famous alternative space/art center in the Washington area. For years now, it has enjoyed a national reputation for providing a forum for new work in relatively experimental and/or interdisciplinary forms, including installations, video, and performance art. Social and aesthetic issues are often addressed.

In its current location, WPA breathes with 8,000 sq. ft. and 13-foot ceilings. The early directors and members were largely responsible for the redevelopment of that particular city block, now known as Gallery Row or Gallery Place.

WPA offers an excellent art bookstore called Bookworks. Some of the best periodicals, books, treatises, freebies, even limited edition artists' books are available, as well as New Age and European music recordings.

Another WPA program, Botswana, offers occasional evening fellowship for artists. It serves as a minimally structured forum where artists can congregate, socialize, intellectualize, and share each other's new work. Finally, the annual fundraising auction always offers good works of art by some of the area's finest artists.

WASHINGTON SQUARE

1050 Connecticut Avenue, N.W.
Washington, DC 20036
(202)387-3800
Monday-Saturday 10-8, Sunday 12-5

Director: Elena Canavier
Sales referred to artist
Established 1984

While not exactly an art center, Washington Square is a good place to see consistently high quality sculpture, including much large-scale work.

Washington Square provides exhibition space in the form of three storeys of a public lobby for Washington area sculptors. Either Elena Canavier Associates curates the exhibits, or area-wide juried competitions are held. No fees or commissions are charged.

Sculptors interested in participating are encouraged to write to Washington Square and ask to be placed on the mailing list for calls for entry. Enclosing slides is recommended in the event that curated exhibitions are organized.

WASHINGTON STUDIO SCHOOL

Please see Circle Gallery, profiled earlier in this chapter.

WASHINGTON WOMEN'S ART CENTER

Please see The New Art Center, profiled earlier in this chapter.

College and University Art Galleries

AMERICAN UNIVERSITY. Watkins Art Gallery, 4400 Massachusetts Avenue, N.W., Washington, DC 20016, (202)885-1670. Monday-Friday 10-12 and 1-4, Saturday 1-4.

CATHOLIC UNIVERSITY OF AMERICA. Salve Regina Gallery, 620 Michigan Avenue, N.E., Washington, DC 20064, (202)635-5282. Monday-Friday 9-5.

GEORGE WASHINGTON UNIVERSITY. Dimock Gallery, Lower Lisner Auditorium, 730 21st Street, N.W., Washington, DC 20052, (202)994-7091. Tuesday-Friday 10-5, Saturday 12-5. Colonnade Gallery, Marvin Center, Third Floor, 800 21st Street, N.W., Washington, DC 20052, (202)994-9188. Sunday-Saturday 10-7.

HOWARD UNIVERSITY. Gallery of Art, College of Fine Arts, 2455 6th Street, N.W., Washington, DC 20059, (202)636-7070. Monday-Friday 9-4:30.

MARYLAND COLLEGE OF ART AND DESIGN. Gudelsky Gallery, 10500 Georgia Avenue, Silver Spring, MD 20902, (301)649-4454. Monday-Friday 10-4:30.

MONTGOMERY COLLEGE Rockville Campus Art Gallery, 51 Manakee Street (at Route 355), Rockville, MD 20850, (301)279-5115. Monday, Thursday, and Friday 9-4:30, Tuesday and Wednesday 9-9, Saturday 11-2. Takoma Park Pavilion of Fine Arts, Takoma Avenue and Fenton Street, Takoma Park, MD 20912, (301)587-4090, x.282. Monday-Friday 9-4.

MOUNT VERNON COLLEGE. Gatehouse Gallery, 2100 Foxhall Road, N.W., Washington, DC 20007, (202)331-0400 and (202)331-3500. Sunday-Saturday 8-4.

NORTHERN VIRGINIA COMMUNITY COLLEGE. Tyler Gallery, 3001 North Beauregard Street, Alexandria, VA 22311, (703)845-6273 and (703)845-6244. Monday-Friday 8:30-8.

PRINCE GEORGE'S COMMUNITY COLLEGE. Marlboro Gallery, 301 Largo Road, Largo, MD 20785, (301)322-0965. Monday-Friday 9-4.

UNIVERSITY OF THE DISTRICT OF COLUMBIA. Gallery 900, 916 G Street, N.W., Washington, DC 20001, (202)727-2662. Hours vary; call first.

UNIVERSITY OF MARYLAND. Art Gallery, Art and Sociology Building, Room 2202, College Park, MD 20742, (301)454-2763. Monday-Friday 10-4, Wednesday until 9, Saturday-Sunday 1-5. Parents Association Art Gallery, Adele H. Stamp Union, College Park, MD 20742, (301)454-4753. Monday-Saturday 8-8, Sunday 12-8.

Alternative Spaces

ART IN EMBASSIES. U.S. Department of State, Art in Embassies Program, A/FBO/ART, Room B-258, Washington, DC 20520, (202)647-5723. Exhibits in U.S. embassies abroad.

ARTS CLUB OF WASHINGTON. 2017 Eye Street, N.W., Washington, DC 20006, (202)331-7282. Membership organization/club. Exhibitions, special events, studios.

ARTS IN THE ACADEMY. National Academy of Sciences, 2101 Constitution Avenue, N.W., Washington, DC 20037, (202)334-2439. Arts related to any of the natural and physical sciences; may incorporate natural elements, electronics, computers, etc.

BRAZILIAN-AMERICAN CULTURAL INSTITUTE. 4103 Connecticut Avenue, N.W., Washington, DC, 20008, (202)362-8334.

CAPITAL GALLERY. *Capital Gallery, located in the Capital Centre, is administered by Montpelier Cultural Arts Center, profiled in the Art Centers chapter.*

CHILDREN'S HOSPITAL. 111 Michigan Avenue, N.W., Washington, DC 20017, (202)745-3225. Exhibits.

THE COLLECTOR. 1630 U Street, N.W., Washington, DC 20009, (202)745-1825. This restaurant and gallery sponsors high-quality changing and, so far, ambitious exhibitions. They hope to become the meeting place for all art lovers—artists, dealers, collectors.

DISTRICT CREATIVE (D.C.) SPACE. 443 7th Street, N.W., Washington, DC 20004, (202)347-4960. This nightclub sponsors regular exhibitions alongside the most contemporary of musical performances.

DUMBARTON CONCERT GALLERY. 3133 Dumbarton Street, N.W., Washington, DC 20007, (202)965-2000. Regular exhibitions. Open during concerts.

FRIENDSHIP GALLERY. Friendship Heights Community Center, 4433 S. Park Avenue, Chevy Chase, MD 20815, (301)656-2797. Exhibitions.

GEORGE MEANY CENTER FOR LABOR STUDIES. 10000 New Hampshire Avenue, Silver Spring, MD 20903, (301)431-6400. Exhibitions.

GEORGETOWN UNIVERSITY HOSPITAL. 3800 Reservoir Road, N.W., Washington, DC 20007, (202)625-7683.

GOLDMAN GALLERY. *Please refer to Jewish Community Center of Greater Washington, listed below.*

GREAT FALLS PARK. 9200 Old Dominion Drive, Great Falls, VA 22066, (703)759-2169. Exhibitions of art with nature themes.

INTER-AMERICAN DEVELOPMENT BANK. Staff Association Art Gallery, 801 17th Street, N.W., Washington, DC 20577. Exhibitions of work by artists from member countries.

INTERNATIONAL MONETARY FUND SOCIETY. The Arts Society, 700 19th Street, N.W., Washington, DC 20431, (202)623-7799. Exhibitions.

JEWISH COMMUNITY CENTER OF GREATER WASHINGTON. 6125 Montrose Road, Rockville, MD 20852, (301)881-0100. Exhibits, classes, workshops, lectures.

LEE ARTS CENTER. 5722 Lee Highway, Arlington, VA 22207, (703)538-5607. Arts activities include visual arts. Classes, workshops, exhibitions.

MARTIN LUTHER KING LIBRARY (LIBRARY FOR THE ARTS). 901 G Street, N.W., Washington, DC 20001, (202)737-1331. This D.C. public library is a library for the arts. Exhibit space in the form of three galleries on a lower level is available to visual artists.

MCLEAN COMMUNITY CENTER. 1234 Ingleside Avenue, McLean, VA 22101, (703)790-9248. Classes, exhibitions.

OMNI GEORGETOWN HOTEL. 2121 P Street, N.W., Washington, DC 20037. Phillips Ballroom and Café Beaux Arts both offer admirable exhibition programs with alot of technical assistance and support.

ORGANIZATION OF AMERICAN STATES GALLERY. 17th and Constitution Avenue, N.W., Washington, DC 20006, (202)789-3000. Exhibitions of artwork by Latin-American artists.

RAYWORKS GALLERY. Takoma Metro Arts Center, 6925 Willow Street, N.W., Washington, DC 20012, (202)291-0728. Although this is primarily a shop, carrying furniture and objects, they exhibit artwork as well.

SIDWELL FRIENDS DAY SCHOOL. Daryl Reich Rubenstein Gallery, Kogod Arts Center, 3825 Wisconsin Avenue, N.W., Washington, DC 20016. This beautiful gallery sponsors regular exhibits.

CHARLES SUMNER SCHOOL MUSEUM AND ARCHIVES. 17th and M Streets, N.W., Washington, DC 20036. Exhibitions.

U.S. GEOLOGICAL SURVEY. 12201 Sunrise Valley Drive, Reston, VA 22092, (703)648-5651. Exhibitions.

VIRGINIA THEOLOGICAL SEMINARY. 3737 Seminary Road, Alexandria, VA 22304, (703)370-6600. Exhibitions.

WESLEY THEOLOGICAL SEMINARY. 4500 Massachusetts Avenue, N.W., Washington, DC 20016, (202)885-8600. Exhibitions, residencies for artists.

WORTHY GALLERY. 1020 29th Street, N.W., Washington, DC 20007, (202)342-0101. Worthy Gallery, a non-profit arm of the Washington Women's Professional Women's Cooperative, offers alternative gallery space for women artists.

ART CONSULTANTS

NOTE: *Almost every commercial gallery, whether they handle contemporary or historical art, offers extensive art consulting services.*
The firms profiled in this section call themselves art consultants, not galleries, although many of them maintain showrooms open by appointment. Services offered by art consultants generally include: (1) working as a broker between artist and client commissioning one or more site-specific works of art; usually all steps of the process are handled by the consultant, from proposing artist(s) to the installation of the artwork(s); (2) assisting client in locating work which is already in existence—one or more specific works, work by specific artists, or work in certain styles or media—or curating an entire collection; (3) installation or framing advice, ranging from suggestions to the carrying out of the job; (4) supplying temporary art for special events.

ART ADVISORY SERVICES, INC.

2883 Audubon Terrace, N.W.
Washington, DC 20008
(202)244-2472
By appointment

President: Vivienne M. Lassman
Cash, check, Visa, MasterCard, American Express, payment plan
Established 1983

Art Advisory Services, Inc. (AASI) specializes in providing artwork by Washington area artists. Most media and styles are in the slide registry or can be located. Commissions are frequently arranged. Auxiliary services include slide presentations, the supplying of artwork for special events, framing and installation of artwork, and the development of collections for both private and corporate clients.

Artists interested in being considered for AASI's slide registry may send a letter with slides and a resumé. Artists are added based primarily on originality, proficiency of technique, and consistency.

THE ART SOURCE, INC.

1120 20th Street, N.W., Suite 205
Washington, DC 20036
(202)429-9270
Monday-Friday 9-4:30 by appointment
Member American Society of Appraisers

Partners: Laura Kaufman, Sandra Tropper
Cash, check, payment plan
Established 1981

Specializing in abstract art, The Art Source usually works with the trade: developers, designers, architects and corporations. Projects range from art for a residence or an entire building, to major outdoor sculpture installations. Art Source will also work with private collectors to locate works by a particular artist.

Work by "several hundred" artists from the U.S. and Europe is available, in two- and three-dimensional media including the traditional as well as the unusual such as handmade paper or artists' books.

Artists interested in being on file are welcome to send a letter with slides and resumé or call for an appointment; artists are tried out based on professionalism of presentation and saleability.

ARTISTS CIRCLE, LTD.

11544 Spring Ridge Road
Potomac, MD 20854
(301)921-0572
Monday-Friday 9-5 by appointment

Owner/Director: Sharon Buchanan
Cash, check
Established 1972

Artists Circle features a 1,000 sq. ft. showroom where the work of hundreds of artists can be seen either in original or slide form. Paintings, sculpture, photography, signed offsets, and fine crafts including ceramics and tapestry are offered in traditional, representational, impressionist, abstract and abstract-expressionist styles. Commissions can be arranged.

Artists interested in registering with Artists Circle may send a letter with slides and resumé or call for an appointment. Artists are chosen based on originality, proficiency of technique, saleability, and scale of work in relation to the site for which the art is being commissioned.

ARTSPACE ENTERPRISES

2025 Rosemont Avenue, N.W.
Washington, DC 20010
(202)667-6610
Monday-Friday 9-6 by appointment

Owner/Director: Richard Griffith Williams
Cash, check, payment plan
Established 1982

ARTSPACE Enterprises deals in paintings, drawings, collage, signed offsets, and sculpture. Established and emerging professional artists from the Washington area and nationwide are represented; their styles include representational and abstract. Commissions can be arranged.

Richard Williams is not currently interested in reviewing additional portfolios.

AVIO GALLERIES, INC.

23485 L'Enfant Plaza, S.W.
Washington, DC 20026
(202)289-1112
By appointment

Owners: Monica Lesko (Director)
and Frank de Serio
Cash, check, MasterCard, Visa, payment plan
Established 1974

Avio Galleries, Inc., also known as Corporate Art Services, Inc., Art for Interiors, and Art for Health Services, was set up to provide "timeless images for corporate environments." Representational and abstract works are immediately available, and commissions can be arranged in all media from paintings and drawings to architectural ornamentation/outdoor sculpture, original prints, and crafts. Some unsigned offsets are also available.

Artists interested in being on file in the slide resource may send a letter with slides. Consistency, technique, and volume of work are factors of selection.

BARNUM/PEABODY ART

1765 P Street, N.W.
Washington, DC 20036
(202)387-3877
Monday-Friday 9-5 by appointment

Partners: Nancy Barnum and Pamela Peabody
Cash, check, payment plan
Established 1984

Associated with Art Placement International in New York, Nancy Barnum and Pamela Peabody call themselves "art advisors and finders." Specializing in 20th century art, they have extensive files of emerging artists in the Washington area and nationwide. Besides working with architects, designers, and developers to find art for public spaces and offices, they also advise corporations and individuals interested in specific work or assembling a collection.

Artists interested in having slides on file may send a letter with slides and a resumé or phone for an appointment. Artists are chosen primarily based on originality, proficiency of technique, and consistency.

CHARLES BARRY INTERNATIONAL

7315 Wisconsin Avenue, Suite 727-E
Bethesda, MD 20814
(301)986-1288
Tuesday-Saturday by appointment

Owner/Director: Charles Goldstein
Cash, check, Visa, MasterCard,
American Express
Established 1975

Charles Barry International carries primarily prints in editions of all sizes, but also handles paintings, sculpture, and some wearable art. Artists include Erté, Nieman, Barnet, Rothe, Yamagata, Agam.

Charles Goldstein is not currently interested in seeing new portfolios.

JEAN EFRON/ART CONSULTANTS

2440 Virginia Avenue, N.W., Suite 1210
Washington, DC 20037
(202)223-1626
Monday-Friday 9-5 by appointment

Owner/Director: Jean Efron
Cash, check
Established 1974

Jean Efron works with artists and dealers throughout the United States and abroad. She says, "As an art consultant, we must be able to present work in all areas; we do not exclusively represent any artist or type of art. We are independent consultants able to show art of all kinds to clients." Efron's clients are primarily corporate collectors, designers, architects, and developers.

Auxiliary services include slide presentations, assistance in building a collection, the arranging of tours, and the producing of catalogs. Assistance with custom framing and installation is also offered.

Artists are welcome to send slides and a resumé.

GUGGENHEIM-MANNES

(202)543-9226
By appointment

Partners: Shelly Guggenheim and Judy Mannes

Shelly Guggenheim and Judy Mannes specialize in contemporary work in media including paintings, drawings, sculpture, site-specific installations, original prints, and fine crafts in glass, clay, wood, and metal. Work by both established and emerging artists can be located for the client. Specialized requests, i.e. for mainstream art by handicapped artists, or by artists from specific geographical areas, are always welcome. Guggenheim-Mannes' clients are corporate and private.

Guggenheim says, "We are happy to curate shows or help organize them in other ways."

The firm is always interested in artists, who are encouraged to send slides and supporting materials.

INNER-VISIONS

Please see the Contemporary Galleries chapter.

INTERIOR MOTIVES

2 Vineyard Haven Ct.
Gaithersburg, MD 20879
(301)670-1776
Monday-Friday 8-5:30 by appointment

Owner/Director: Nancie M. Booth
Cash, check
Established 1981

Interior Motives handles representational, impressionist, abstract, oriental, and western art in the forms of paintings, sculpture, photography, and prints from hand-pulled to unsigned offsets.

Artists interested in being associated with Interior Motives may send a letter with slides, or phone for an appointment to show actual work.

BONNIE KENNY, INC.

2301 Connecticut Avenue, N.W.
Washington, DC 20008
(202)328-9505
By appointment

Owner: Bonnie Kenny
Cash, check

Bonnie Kenny believes that "the core of any room rests with its fine art." She will locate art of any medium and time period. In fact, she likes to weave many different kinds of art into a nonetheless cohesive collection where period and place of origin do not matter.

SHERLEY KOTEEN ASSOCIATES

2604 Tilden Street, N.W.
Washington, DC 20008
(202)363-2233
By appointment

Director: Shirley Koteen

Sherley Koteen is capable of locating any kind of contemporary by a great number of artists. However, her special area of expertise is in contemporary fine crafts. She has sources nationwide including leading craft artists and dealers.

H. H. LEONARDS, INC.

2020 O Street, N.W.
Washington, DC 20036
(202)659-8787
By appointment

Owner/Director: H. H. Leonards
Cash, check, Visa, MasterCard, American Express, payment plan
Established 1980

H. H. Leonards specializes in designing and carrying out art programs, usually for corporate environments. She has experience in many such programs including art investment, public exhibition, and fundraising. Leonards believes that bringing artwork into offices contributes to the daily lives of the people who work there, and she also feels that art can be a powerful image-building tool. If a client is not ready to invest, the leasing of artwork can be arranged. Installation and framing is available too.

Leonards has on hand an eclectic mix of pieces in a four-story brownstone near Dupont Circle; over 5,000 pieces of art, antiques and collectibles are available. Paintings, drawings, sculpture, photography, prints from signed originals to posters, wearables, collage, fine crafts, even puppets, are available. Almost everything is for sale.

Artists interested in having their work considered may send a letter with slides, recommendations and a resumé. New artists are chosen primarily based on originality, proficiency of technique, and professionalism.

OCTOGENY

10404 Lloyd Road
Potomac, MD 20854
(301)340-0143
By appointment

Owner/Director: Phyllis Beek
Cash, check
Established 1981

Octogeny provides art consulting services to the trade, as well as to corporations and private collectors throughout the country.

In addition to a large inventory of art in Potomac, Phyllis Beek has sources for published and original art nationwide and in Europe. She has on hand an extensive slide and photo registry of artists' and publishers' inventory.

All media are available and/or can be commissioned.

PORTRAIT CONNECTION
[See Color Plate after page 64]

4101 Legation Street, N.W.
Washington, DC 20015
(202)244-4693
By appointment

Owner/Director: Lorraine Arden
Cash, check, payment plan
Established 1986

Lorraine Arden, co-author of this book, is an artist herself. She saw the need for a portrait agency which would represent a wider variety of media and styles than is normally available. Portrait Connection specializes in representing Washington area artists—established career portraitists as well as emerging artists—chosen for their ability both to create unusual art and to achieve likenesses. Media range from traditional oil painting to sculptural media and even original prints and other works on paper. Styles run the gamut: realist, photo-realist, impressionist, naive, somewhat abstract, and pop. Family, executive, and informal portraits, as well as unique portraits in an artist's distinctive style, are available, from $100-20,000.

Artists interested in being considered may call for an appointment or send a letter with slides and resumé. New artists are chosen based primarily on proficiency of technique, originality of vision, and saleability. Group shows are sponsored in Washington area art spaces once or twice yearly.

THE PORTRAIT GROUP

125 N. Lee Street, #408
Alexandria, VA 22314
(703)836-2287
Monday-Saturday by appointment

Owner/Director: Pat Young Hallgren
Cash, check, payment plan
Established 1987

The Portrait Group serves as a broker for 15 portrait artists. Portfolio books are available for viewing past works done in traditional manners in oils, watercolor, pastel, drawings, sculpture, and photography. Some of the artists represented include John Howard Sanden, Raymond Kinstler, and others. Prices range from $2,000-$30,000.

Artists interested in representation may send a letter with slides and a resumé. New artists are chosen primarily based on consistency and education.

PORTRAIT REPRESENTATIVES, INC.

3910 Livingston Street, N.W.
Washington, DC 20015
(202)966-0446
By appointment

Partners: Mary Boudreau (Director)
and Michele Broadfoot
Cash, check, payment plan
Established 1986

Portrait Representatives, Inc. is a fine arts brokerage firm dealing exclusively in portraiture. Established professional portrait artists in the Washington area and nationwide can achieve likenesses in oils, watercolor, pastel, or sculpture. Executive, family, and informal portraits as well as pet and residential portraits are handled. In an effort to make commissioning a portrait enjoyable and effortless, Mary Boudreau and Michele Broadfoot enjoy helping clients select the appropriate artist and medium.
Portrait Representatives, Inc. is not currently interested in handling additional artists.

HOLLY ROSS ASSOCIATES

Please see the Contemporary Galleries section.

SAINDON & SELIGMANN FINE ART SERVICES, INC.

1020 19th Street, N.W.
Washington, DC 20036
(202)223-4121
Monday-Friday 8:30-5:30 by appointment

Partners: Catherine Saindon and Monica Seligmann
Cash, check, payment plan
Established 1982

Saindon & Seligmann Fine Art Services, Inc. is a corporate consulting firm, working with businesses, developers, hotels, and hospitals. Projects of any scale are welcome; prices range from $100 to $50,000 and media include paintings, drawings, sculpture, photography, original prints, wearable art, fine crafts, and offsets. Artists in all phases of their careers and of many nationalities are represented. An extensive client/reference list is available for those interested in contracting with Saindon & Seligmann.
Artists wishing to be considered may send a letter with recommendations, slides and a resumé, or call for an appointment. New artists are chosen primarily based on saleability, proficiency of technique, and professionalism. Saindon & Seligmann also sponsors changing exhibition programs in corporate settings, such as the Artists in the Atrium juried shows installed at the Times Journal Co.

Untitled, 1987, by John Roper. Black iron with copper rods, 30" in height. Sardi Associates, Inc.

SARDI ASSOCIATES, INC.

7819 Butterfield Lane
Annandale, VA 22003
(703)573-0010
By appointment

Owner/Director: Sardi Snyder
Cash, check
Established 1980

    Sardi Snyder's services include research and consultation; planning and selection; archival framing/mounting; delivery and installation. Several media are available: original paintings on canvas and paper, original prints, fiber pieces, shadow designs, hand-made paper, and photography. However, Snyder's main expertise is sculpture in metals as well as marble, stone, acrylic, and mixed materials. To achieve a stated goal of offering artwork which is distinctive to the area, Snyder exclusively represents several artists both established and emerging. In fact, she is set up also to act as an artist agent in certain cases—in a profession generally catering to the client, this extra offer to artists, while not offered free of charge, is somewhat unusual.

    Artists interested in Sardi Associates' services may send a letter with recommendations, slides and a resumé, or call for an appointment.

SCULPTURE PLACEMENT

P.O. Box 9709
Washington, DC 20016
(202)362-9310
By appointment

Director: Paula Stoeke
Established 1981

Sculpture Placement is a Washington based organization which curates and coordinates travelling exhibitions of outdoor sculpture. Recent exhibition sites include: The World Trade Center, New York; Warner Communications, New York; Washington Harbour, Washington, D.C.; Energy Center, New Orleans; Yale University; and corporate development projects for the Trammell Crow Company, Property Company of America, and Lincoln Property Company.

In addition, Sculpture Placement is the exclusive representative for the work of J. Seward Johnson, Jr. worldwide; an example of Johnson's work is on the cover of this book. Commissions can be arranged.

SCULPTURE SOURCE

International Sculpture Center
1050 Potomac Street, N.W.
Washington, DC 20007
(202)965-6066
Monday-Friday 9-5

Director: Laurie Stinson
Cash, check, Visa, MasterCard, American Express
Established 1986

International Sculpture Center is a non-profit membership organization; artist dues are currently $35. Services to artists include the availability of group insurance, a subscription to *International Sculpture* magazine, and inclusion in the slide registry. Or, a sculptor may register his/her slides for $15 and forego the other benefits.

Founded by artists and arts managers, ISC was set up primarily to market and promote contemporary sculptors—to serve as a broker linking artists with those who wish to exhibit or purchase art. ISC works with developers, architects, interior designers, art consultants, and others. Their data base contains thousands of works which are cross-referenced through variables including size, medium, subject matter, cost, and location. Because ISC eventually expanded to offer so many diverse services, Sculpture Source is the name of the arm of ISC operating as a sculpture broker.

Other services offered are lectures, slide presentations, organization/coordination of sculpture competitions of any scope, negotiation of loans of artworks, and maintenance/conservation.

Artists interested in joining the registry may write to the above address for membership information and forms.

NICKI SHEARER ART SOURCE

Bethesda, MD
(301)320-2210
By appointment only

Owner/Director: Nicki Shearer
Cash, check
Established 1979

Nicki Shearer works primarily with corporate and commercial clients wishing to put quality artwork into public spaces. Representing a diverse selection of local and national artists with established reputations, works range from small prints to large sculpture pieces and large fiber works. Shearer often works with artists to arrange commissions of site-specific pieces. Assistance in framing and installation is offered.

Artists interested in working with Nicki Shearer may call for an appointment.

FRANÇOISE YOHALEM

6600 Selkirk Drive
Bethesda, MD 20817
(301)229-4645
By appointment

Owner/Director: Françoise Yohalem
Established 1982

Françoise Yohalem specializes in art-in-architecture and public art projects; she works with developers and architects. Helping them find artists who can be commissioned to create site-specific works, she gets involved in the planning stage, sets up a process to find an appropriate artist (sometimes through a competition), and provides coordination and guidance through the installation phase. She maintains a slide registry of artists nationwide who are experienced in large-scale architectural works.

Artists wishing to be considered for future projects may send a letter with slides and a resumé. New artists are chosen primarily based on the ability to create relatively large-scale site-specific works.

INDEX

A Salon, Ltd., 74
Aaron Gallery, 13
Adams Davidson Gallery, 102
Adamson Gallery, David, 14
Addison/Ripley Gallery, 15
Affrica, 113
AFR Fine Art, 16
Alex Gallery, 17
Alpha Gallery, 18
Alternative Spaces, 155
Americana West Gallery, 18
Anacostia Neighborhood Museum, 119
Andreas Galleries, 19
Anton Gallery, 20
Ardel Gallery, 21
Arlington Arts Center, 145
Art Advisory Services, Inc., 161
Art Barn, 145
Art Centers, 144
Art Consultants, 159
Art in Embassies, 156
Art Gallery (University of Maryland), 154
Art League, 146
Art Source, 162
Art Unlimited, 94
Artists Circle, Ltd., 162
Arts Club of Washington, 156
Arts in the Academy, 156
Artspace Enterprises, 162
Athenaeum, 146
Atlantic Gallery, 22
Avio Galleries, Inc., 162
Bader Fine Arts Limited, Virginia, 94
Bader Gallery, Franz, 23
Barnes Gallery, 103
Barney Studio House, 119
Barnum/Peabody Fine Arts, 163
Barry International, Charles, 163
Baumgartner Galleries Inc., 24

Berler, Dealer Fine Photographic Prints, Sandra, 25
Bethesda Art Gallery, 103
Bird-in-Hand Gallery and Bookstore, 25
Bishop's Gallery, 95
Brazilian-American Cultural Institute, 156
Brody's Gallery, 26
Brown Contemporary Art, Robert, 27
Buffalo Gallery, 27
Café de Beaux Arts, 157
Calvert Gallery, 103
Capital Gallery, 148
Capricorn Galleries, 28-29
Carega Gallery, Patricia, 30
Chalkley Galleries, Jackie, 87
Cherub Gallery, 104
Children's Hospital, 156
Circle Gallery, 147
City Gallery, 74
Collector, The, 156
College and University Art Galleries, 153
Colonnade Gallery (George Washington University), 154
Contemporary Art, Commercial Galleries, 12
Contemporary Art, Cooperative Galleries, 73
Contemporary Functional Art, 86
Contemporary Multiples, 93
Cooperative Galleries, 73
Corcoran Gallery of Art, 120-21
Damon Galleries, Ltd., 95
Dimock Gallery (George Washington University), 154
District Creative Space, 156

Dumbarton Concert Gallery, 156
Dumbarton Oaks, 122
Efron/Art Consultants, Jean, 163
Ernst Alexander Gallery, 31
Evans-Tibbs Collection, 122
Ewing Gallery, Kathleen, 32
Fendrick Gallery, 33
Fisher Galleries, 34
Fondo del Sol, 123
Foreword, 6
Foundry Gallery, 75
Foxhall Gallery, 34
Foxley/Leach Gallery, 35
Freer Gallery of Art, 124-125
Friendship Gallery, 156
Galerie Lareuse, 36
Galerie Triangle, 37
Gallerie Julian, 96
Gallerie La Taj, 113
Gallery 4, 37
Gallery 10, 76-77
Gallery 900 (University of the District of Columbia), 154
Gallery K, 38
Gallery by Lee, 87
Gallery of Art (Howard University), 154
Gallery Lafayette, 104
Gallery West, 78
Gatehouse Gallery (Mount Vernon College), 154
George Meany Center for Labor Studies, 156
Georgetown Fine Arts, 96
Georgetown Gallery of Art, 105
Georgetown University Hospital, 156
Gilpin Gallery, 39
Glass Gallery, 40
Glen Echo Gallery, 147
Goldman Gallery, 156
Govinda Gallery, 41
Great Falls Park, 156
Greater Reston Arts Center (GRACE), 147

Green Spring Gallery, 148
Guarisco Gallery, 105
Gudelsky Gallery (Maryland College of Art and Design), 154
Guggenheim-Mannes, 164
Harmattan, 113
Haslem Gallery, Jane, 42
Hendricks Art Collection, Ltd., 114
Henri Gallery, 43
Hensley Gallery, 97
Heritage Gallery of Classical Realism, 44
Herndon Old Town Gallery, 79
Hillwood, 126
Hirshhorn Museum and Sculpture Garden, 126
Historical Art, Commercial Galleries, 101
Hom Gallery, 106
Images International, 97
Inner-Visions of Georgetown, 45
Inter-American Development Bank, 156
Interior Motives, 164
International Monetary Fund Society, 156
Introduction for the Artist, 9
Introduction for the Collector, 7
Jewish Community Center of Greater Washington, 157
Jones Troyer, 46
Kenny, Bonnie, Inc., 164
Kimberly Gallery of Art, 47
King Street Antiques, 106
Kleinman, R.I.B.A. Gallery, Patricia, 107
Kornblatt Gallery, B. R., 48
Koteen & Associates, Sherley, 165
Lee Arts Center, 157
Leonards, Inc., H. H., 165
Library of Congress, 127

Library for the Arts, 157
Liros Gallery, Inc., 108
Littleton Gallery, 49
Marlboro Gallery (Prince George's Community College), 154
Martin Gallery, 49
Martin Luther King Library, 157
Mateyka Gallery, Marsha, 50
McIntosh/Drysdale, 51
McLean Community Center, 157
Mickelson Gallery, 52
Middendorf Gallery, 53
Mogul Gallery, 88
Montpelier Cultural Arts Center, 148
Moon, Blossoms and Snow, 88
Morris Fine Arts, Marilyn, 89
Museum of Modern Art in Latin America, 127
Museums, 117
National Air and Space Museum, 127
National Gallery of Art, 128
National Gallery of Art, East Wing, 128-129
National Museum of African Art, 130-131
National Museum of American Art, 132-133
National Museum of American History, 134
National Museum of Women in the Arts, 134-135
National Portrait Gallery, 136
New Art Center, 149
Newman Gallery, 54
Ninth Street Gallery, 54
Nuñez Gallery, Angel, 108
O'Brien Gallery, Anne, 55-56
Octogeny, 165
Old Mill Gallery, 80
Old Print Gallery, 108
Old Warsaw Galleries, 57

Omni Georgetown Hotel, 157
Organization of American States Gallery, 157, and *see* Museum of Modern Art in Latin America
Original Accents, 90
Osuna Gallery, 58
Other Cultures, Commercial Galleries, 112
P & C Art, Inc., 98
Parents Association Art Gallery (University of Maryland), 154
Partners Gallery, 59
Paul VI Institute for the Arts, 150
Pavo Real, 98
Pensler, Inc., Alan, 109
Phillips Collection, 136-137
Picturesque, 60
Pirjo, 90
Plum Gallery, 60
Portrait Connection, 166
Portrait Group, 166
Portrait Representatives, Inc., 167
Prince Royal Gallery, 99
R Street Gallery, *see* A Salon, Ltd.
Rayworks Gallery, 157
Regency Gallery, Inc., 61
Renwick Gallery, 138-139
Rockville Campus Art Gallery (Montgomery College), 154
Ross Associates Gallery, Holly, 61
Sackler Gallery, Arthur M., 140-141
Saindon & Seligmann, 167
St. Luke's Gallery, 109
Salve Regina Gallery (Catholic University), 154
Sander Fine Art, 114
Sansar, 91
Sardi Associates, Inc., 168

Schweitzer Japanese Prints Inc., 114
Sculpture Placement, 169
Sculpture Source, 169
Seidner Gallery, 110
Shainman Gallery, Jack, 62
Shearer, Nicki, 170
Shogun Gallery, 115
Sidwell Friends Day School, 157
Spectrum Gallery, 81
Strathmore Hall Arts Center, 150
Studio Antiques, Inc., 110
Studio Gallery, 82-83
Sumner School Museum and Archives, Charles, 157
Taggart, Jorgensen & Putman, 111
Takoma Metro Arts Center, *See* A Salon, New Art Center
Takoma Park Pavilion of Fine Arts (Montgomery College), 154
Tartt Gallery, 63
Textile Museum, 142
Torpedo Factory Art Center, 151
Touchstone Gallery, 83-84
Town Center Gallery, 84
Tribes, 115
Trocadéro, 115
Trocadéro Textile Art, 116
Tyler Gallery (Northern Virginia Community College), 154
U. S. Geological Survey, 157
University and College Art Galleries, 153
Uptown Arts, 99
Veerhoff Galleries, 64
Venable Neslage Galleries, 65
Veni Vidi Vici, 91
Village Gallery of Great Falls, 65
Virginia Theological Seminary, 157
VO Galerie, 92
Volta Place, *see* Affrica
Walker, Ursitti & McGinniss Gallery, 66
Wallace Wentworth Gallery, 67-68
Washington Gallery of Fine Arts, 69
Washington Printmakers Gallery, 85
Washington Project for the Arts (WPA), 152
Washington Square, 152
Washington Women's Art Center, *see* New Art Center
Watergate Gallery, 69
Watkins Art Gallery (American University), 154
Willow Street Gallery, *see* Takoma Metro Arts Center
Winston Gallery, 70
Worthy Gallery, 157
Yohalem, Françoise, 170
Zenith Gallery, 71
Zygos Gallery, 72